Here and Now
STITCHERY
from Other Times and Places

ROBBIE and TONY FANNING

Here and Now STITCHERY from Other Times and Places

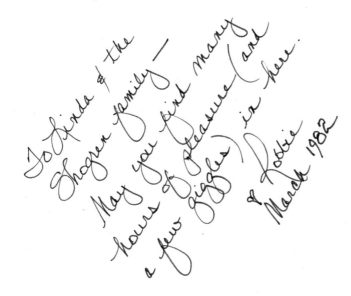

To Linda of the Shogren family —
May you find many
hours of pleasure (and
a few giggles) in here.
♥ Robbie
March 1982

Butterick Publishing

for my father, J. Edwin Losey: a link
and for my sister, Mary M. Losey
RLF

to my brother, John, whose industry and example
have led me to where I am today
ADF

Library of Congress Catalog Card Number: 77-92586
International Standard Book Number: 0-88421-047-2
Copyright © 1978 by Butterick Publishing
161 Sixth Avenue   New York, New York 10013
A Division of American Can Company

All rights reserved. No part of this book may be repro-
duced in any form or by any electronic or mechanical
means, including information storage and retrieval sys-
tems, without permission in writing from the publisher,
except by a reviewer who may quote brief passages in a
review.

Color photographs by Lars Speyer

Illustrations by Tony Fanning

Book Design by Lucy Bitzer

Black and white photographs by Robbie and
Tony Fanning unless otherwise noted

Printed in the United States of America

CONTENTS

PREFACE

Consider the power of folk embroidery. It makes us stop a stranger on the street to ask where she (or he) got that brightly colored peasant blouse or shirt; and it makes that stranger tell not where the piece was bought, but where it was made, perhaps adding something interesting about the people who made it. Strange, that mere threads arranged on fabric could break down barriers so easily.

What is the source of this power? Is it the texture of the yarn, the colors, the patterns?

No, it is neither materials nor techniques alone that give folk embroidery its impact and beauty. What shines through is the spirit of the makers. The best work was originally done on objects meant to be personally worn or used by its creators, and so it reflects their very lives. If you are going to wear your embroidery before all your friends, or if your husband-to-be is going to wear it at your wedding, naturally you will feel strongly about it. This feeling and care shine through in folk embroidery: "If it's for me and mine, of course I'll make it good."

For this reason, it's often unsatisfying merely to duplicate a folk design from another culture, to copy a baptismal gown or burial wrapping. We strongly feel that adapting the stitchery techniques, designs, and motifs of traditional folk embroidery to those objects that *you* care for, wear, and use will give your work the same power of ethnic embroidery. Our projects are designed with this personal significance in mind, and after you have mastered a technique, take the time to examine what it is of your own you'd like to make beautiful with it. Even if it's only a pair of jogging shorts, now do it your own way.

Our book is organized into five main parts. Each one deals with one of the natural materials traditionally used in folk embroidery: skins, linen, cotton, wool, and silk. Within each part we examine several cultures and how they used these materials. We study the materials, the techniques, and the lives of the creators. Then we provide a project that incorporates and adapts these aspects for our time and culture. Our choices of technique and culture are purely personal, but our aim is to present variety from which you can choose according to your interests.

We hope that you will travel with us across the barriers of time and culture by working the projects in this book that appeal to you. Each piece is complete in its own right, but if you find one that particularly fascinates you, by all means treat it as a sampler and move on from there. Change the colors; leave out a border; add the flowers in your garden; use a different backing material or different thread. You can do what needleworkers throughout history have done: Make it mean something to your own life. Take it, rework it, adapt it, until you have made it your own.

—Robbie and Tony Fanning
Menlo Park, California

INTRODUCTION

Weather made the human race take up needlework.

When you're cold and wet, you cover your body. In prehistoric times people covered themselves with animal pelts, leaves, or flexible bark. Two pelts give more cover than one, so thorns or bone splinters were used to join the skins.

Then, as now, the use of one technique led to experimentation, which led to a new technique. By piercing the thorn or bone that held the skins together, (wo)man devised the first needle and could then lace together the pelts with sinew or animal hair. And that led to attaching beads and shells as ornament, which led to interest in the pattern of the sinew or thread itself, which gave rise to bindings and borders and embroidered surface patterns. It was a long development, and at the end of it humanity had gone beyond merely wanting to keep warm and dry. Thread was used in its own right to beautify fabrics. Embroidery had been born, and the rest is needle-art history.

As anyone who does it knows, embroidery is and always has

been much more than the filling in of a fabric surface with threads. It is working a needlepoint sampler while sitting next to your child healing in the hospital. It is decorating a workshirt with hummingbirds for a lover. It is making something colorful to brighten winter's gray. It is taking those extra steps so that your great-grandchildren will have visible evidence that you cared enough to make your embroidery last 100 years.

Embroidery is an expression of humanity's universal desire to bring beauty and meaning to usefulness.

In more complex times, there have been two major divisions in embroidery, called *great* and *folk*. Folk embroidery is mostly personal, meant for the maker's immediate environment, not mass-produced for the marketplace. The designs are generally tradition-bound, and each symbol and color relates to the needleworker's own culture. The mola of the Cuna Indians is a good example (see section N). Great embroidery is produced for institutions: churches, governments, the military, businesses. It is generally less personal, one-of-a-kind, and changes as life changes. Neither type of needlework is superior to the other; rather they complement and feed each other. And the division into great and folk is, like most, an artificial one. A whole spectrum of embroidery lies between.

In every society a few people have the gift of illuminating the quality of life. We call these special people artists. Pictured throughout this book is the work of ten artists who use fabric and thread as a medium in the greatest of the great tradition. Note the contrast between their work and the folk work pictured in the book.

HOW TO USE THIS BOOK

The designs in this book are more closely linked with folk embroidery. For each technique we tell you something about the culture that produced it and then explain why and how our own designs evolved. In the Working Process of each section we tell you how we did each project. Use this as a take-off point for your own work, either by changing parts of our design or by working the design twice—once our way to learn and once your way to make it personal, as folk embroiderers around the world have always done.

Each of us has a creative streak. Whether you decide to explore your innate creativity or not is your choice. For those who are still unsure about their creative talent, for each technique we've included a section called "Additional Ideas" to help you grow.

The materials of embroidery traditionally used in needlework are skins, linen, wool, cotton, and silk, and our book is divided accordingly. Does this mean you must skip the section on China because you can't afford silk? Definitely not. Use what you have—the joy of embroidery comes when you adapt it to your own life. The same technique of couching that the Chinese used can be done with any thread. Expand your conception of "thread" to anything flexible and longer than it is wide. You'll soon find yourself trying embroidery with sewing machine thread, knitting yarn, a jump rope, the garden hose, telephone cable, and almost anything in between. Similarly, any fabric a needle can pass through is fair game. Feel free to try any technique on any fabric. Again, think of fabric as a system rather than as cloth and you'll expand your horizons. (No, smocking on chicken wire doesn't work.)

We hope you will respond lustily to this book—underline whatever provokes thought, punch holes along the side edges of cartoons to hold your color samples, color in the designs with felt-tipped pens, write to the authors and artists (see Resources—and enclose a pre-addressed, stamped envelope if you want a reply). It's a book meant to be used, shared, and enjoyed.

To clarify the Fanning working process, here is the division of labor. Every part of the making of this book involved us both, but we each do some of the facets better. Tony did all the drawings and a larger share of the designing. Robbie did the final stitching and most of the writing, and we both took and printed photos. Although Tony often took up a needle and thread to test a design, Robbie's the embroidery nut; therefore it seemed pretentious in the text to say "we like to stitch this way."

People who don't embroider are always stupefied at first by the time it takes. If you were to stitch every project in this book, you would need several eight-day weeks of 27-hour days. But this is not an approach conducive to enjoyment. Embroidery is like a good book; you read slowly, savoring each word and losing yourself in the story. When you're done, you feel satisfied and yet a little sad that it's over. Who cares about the time? It's more important to enjoy each step of the way as your work grows from a few threads to a stunning pattern. (However, we have designed some smaller projects that don't take forever.)

BEFORE YOU BEGIN

If you are new to embroidery, please take the time to read this carefully. Embroidery is not difficult, but doing it well requires forethought and planning. Spending hours on a piece only to have it pucker or the colors run in washing is not our idea of fun.

SUPPLIES

Needles: embroidery is sharp; tapestry is blunt.

Needles Basically there are two kinds, those that bring blood and those that don't. The former are called embroidery needles and the latter, tapestry needles. Some people worry too much about needle sizes. If you understand the concept of the needle, you won't panic when all your needles get mixed up, numberless, in your needle-case. The function of a needle is to poke a hole in the fabric big enough to allow the thread to pass through freely. If the eye of the needle is not large enough to make an adequate hole in the fabric, the thread will catch on the edge of the fabric during each stitch and begin to fray. If the *eye* of the needle is too large, it will leave holes in the fabric—which are sometimes desirable, as in Rhodes work (see section D), and sometimes not. If your fabric already has large holes in it, such as aida cloth or needlepoint canvas, you don't need a sharp needle, so you use a blunt tapestry needle. (Naturally these same ideas apply to sewing machine needles.) If you are working with a sharp needle and need a blunt one for a few chores only, like ending off a thread (see Miscellaneous Working Tips), and you're too lazy to change needles, lead with the eye end of the sharp needle. New embroiderers should buy two packages of assorted sized tapestry (18–22) and embroidery (3–10) needles.

 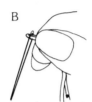 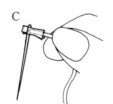 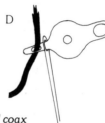

Three ways to thread a needle: A and B. Fold the thread over the needle and coax the folded end through the eye of the needle. C. Fold a small slip of paper or the corner of an envelope over the thread end and push both through the eye. D. The easiest way: use a needle threader.

Experienced needleworkers take for granted even the smallest knowledge. This was brought home when my sister, a librarian, tried to embroider with some teenagers: "We couldn't figure out how to thread the needle at first, but the kids solved it by dipping the end of the yarn in Coke to make it stiff."

Hoops, Frames, and Stretcher Bars After spending many years pooh-poohing hoops and frames in praise of free stitchery, I've become addicted to them. The quality of work done on frames pleases us more than that done free, and we find we can work faster using two hands rather than one that clumsily alternates above and below the material. Those projects in the book that require a frame or hoop are indicated with a ⭕ symbol.

Mail-order sources for hoops, frames, and stretcher bars are in the back of the book.

Fabrics We go into each natural fabric more fully in the beginnings of the five parts of this book. For now, let's just consider thread count and sources.

With respect to the backing material, there are two main categories of embroidery: *geometric* or counted thread, in which threads are worked over a certain number of backing threads; and

In most cases, use a single thread, grasping the short thread end in your pinkie to keep it from slipping out of the needle.

free, in which the weave of the backing fabric makes no difference to the direction of the stitch. Examples of counted thread stitches are cross stitch and blackwork; of free embroidery, chain and buttonhole.

If you are working a counted-thread pattern, you will need an even-weave fabric—that is, a fabric woven with the same number and spacing of warp and weft threads. Some typical even-weave fabrics are Hardanger, aida, even-weave linen, and needlepoint canvas. You may work any counted-thread project on any even-weave fabric (including the screen door); however to duplicate our results, you must work to our specifications—such as 22 threads/ inch Hardanger.

These even-weave fabrics are available in needlework shops (see supply lists). But suppose you want to buy even-weave at your favorite fabric or drapery store. How can you tell if it's precisely woven? One way is to cut off and carry 1″ of a plastic ruler in your purse. Another way is to use a linen tester, which magnifies the threads for easier counting. We bought our linen tester in a photography store, where it is used to read contact prints. Another easy way to count even-weave is to draw an exact 1″ square on an out-of-date credit card, cut out the square with a razor or X-acto knife, and carry the card in your wallet or purse. Lay the 1″ square opening over the fabric, and if there are an equal number of threads in each direction, you're in business. (And if you're more up-to-date than we are, you'll use the metric system.)

Counted thread designs can be worked on any fabric, from felt to leather, with the help of a flimsy white fabric called *waste canvas,* which has colored lines woven in every ten threads to aid in counting. You can also use actual needlepoint canvas (but not interlocking canvas). Baste waste or needlepoint canvas to your fabric and stitch the design over the two, using the threads of the waste canvas to count stitches and taking care not to pierce the threads of the waste canvas. When the embroidery is finished, dampen it with a clean wet sponge. (This means, of course, that your threads and backing material should be color-fast in water.) Remove the threads of the waste canvas with tweezers. Be sure to slide out the canvas threads, so you don't distort your embroidery by lifting or pulling. (The Bulgarian darning project in section F uses waste canvas.)

Waste canvas makes any fabric suitable for counted thread embroidery, and it's especially handy on ready-made clothing, either bought or homemade. Even a simple cross-stitched ladybug on a pocket can give a shirt personality. You can also work simple counted thread designs on regularly patterned fabric like gingham by filling each square with an X.

Testing for even-weave: the view through a linen tester

Hoops, frames, and stretcher bars

Even-weave (clockwise from the linen tester): Hardanger cloth, strap linen, waste canvas, mono canvas, even-weave cotton, penelope canvas, aida (pronounced ah-ee-da or eye-da)

Also, by copying your design onto 10-to-the-inch or smaller graph paper, you can then transfer the design to fabric via carbon paper (see p. 25) and make your own stamped fabric.

There are many mail-order sources for embroidery fabrics, if you can't find them locally. But we hope you won't overlook that all-American folk gathering, the garage sale, as a source of good materials. We've found all types and weights of linen, fantastic wool (passing this life as a coat while it waits to be a pillow), silk, leather, and cotton. If you are not sure of the fiber content, but it's cheap and you like it, buy it and test it when you're home. If the fabric is expensive, try to extract one thread and sneak off to give it a burn test. (And don't give our name when they arrest you for attempted arson.) This is not easy when the purported linen is trapped in a pair of man's golfing shorts.

Burn Tests to Determine Fiber Content

Extract one thread. Hold it over a sink or bowl, preferably with tweezers, and light one end. Observe how quickly it burns and what the ash looks like.

Fiber	Reaction to Flame
cotton and linen	burn rapidly with yellow flame continue to glow after removed from flame leave a soft, gray ash
silk and wool	burn slowly, sizzling and curling away from flame leave a crushable black ash
polyester	burns slowly and shrinks from flame melts and emits black smoke leaves hard black bead
nylon	burns slowly and shrinks from flame melts and leaves a hard gray bead
acrylic	burns and melts both while in flame and after removal leaves a hard, brittle black bead
acetate	burns and melts both while in flame and after removal leaves a hard, brittle black bead smells like vinegar when burning disintegrates when subjected to drop of acetone (nail polish remover)

Another source of fabric, and one too often overlooked, is your local hand weaver. In the past people wove what they needed and could thus produce exactly the type and count of even-weave desired. Today it is exciting to commission hand-woven fabric. For example, wool aida is wonderful to work on but impossible to find. Check with your public library or the telephone book yellow pages for hand weavers.

Threads Anything that goes through a needle can be used as thread, from moosehair to rickrack. In this book, however, we've kept to more mundane thread, like

> embroidery floss
> pearl cotton
> crochet cotton
> linen
> wool
> silk cord
> sewing machine thread

A very general rule is to choose a thread for embroidery that is no bigger than a single thread of your backing fabric. This allows the embroidery thread to pass easily between the fabric threads. Of course, depending on the effect you want, you may wish to violate this rule—in section S, Iran, we use #5 pearl cotton on a fine backing because it lies beautifully on the surface.

To separate the strands of embroidery floss or stranded wool without snarling, put one end in the middle of this (or any other) book and close the book. Keeping a tight tension between the end you're holding and the end in the book, separate as many strands as you need. (You can also hold one end firmly in your lips and separate the thread—but not if you wear lipstick.)

We like to start and end threads with a waste knot. Thread a needle, tie a knot in the end of your thread, and go to the topside of the fabric about 3″ from the place where you want to stitch. As you stitch, the long piece of thread on the back will be covered. When you finish that length of thread, finish with another waste knot. Later you will clip all the knots and pull the thread ends to the back. If they are sufficiently covered not to pull loose, merely clip the exposed thread ends off. If they are not sufficiently covered, thread the loose end on the backside through your needle and slide it under enough stitched work to hold it. Sometimes the thread end is quite short and the needle must be slid under the embroidery *before* threading it. (The tool that's used to repair dropped knitting stitches can also be used to finish short ends.)

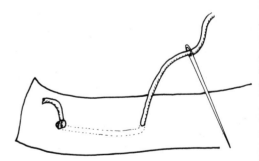

Making a waste knot: Knot the thread and go into the topside of the fabric several inches from the first stitch. When the work has covered the extra thread on the back, cut off the waste knot.

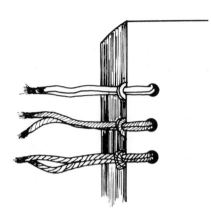

Use this book! Keep your colors coded by punching holes in the margins of the page and writing the dye-lot number and type of thread next to a sample.

Another way to start a thread is to take two or three tiny backstitches where the embroidery will cover it.

Some people, of course, will scoff at this refinement and start and end threads with knots. Five washings of a garment or tablecloth will change your mind as your beautiful work is marred by hanging threads. If you insist on using knots, put a spot of fabric glue on the back—but don't tell any of my stitching friends I told you.

After you buy thread for a project and before you begin stitching, punch holes along the edge of the project cartoon or stitch diagram where the color symbols are. Tie a 3" length of thread into each hole and label the brand and color code number. Then if you should run short of thread, you'll know precisely what color to buy.

There are many systems to organize threads for each project, including a yarn palette (see supply list), but you'll quickly devise your own. I like to knot threads loosely over the round plastic holders of apple juice, soda, or beer six-packs. I also save all the little ends of thread and send them in letters to people I love. Color, no matter how small an amount, brings joy.

How much thread should you buy for your own projects? There is no easy way to estimate, and nothing is more irksome than to run out. If the design calls for heavy stitching, you may need as much as two lengths (about 18" long) per square inch. Each project in this book states how much thread was used. The experience of working these projects will guide you in buying threads for your own work.

We have listed supply sources in two ways: companies that specialize in one product are listed in the Supplies and Bibliography that follow each major part—for example, a source of shisha mirrors (used in Section L, India) is found in the Supplies and Bibliography—Cotton section; companies that carry more than one product are listed in Another Mail Order Supply List at the end of the book.

Sewing Machine Somehow the sewing machine is not associated with ethnic embroidery, and yet all over the world it is used, and often, in clever ways. Do you need a fancy zigzag machine? Most certainly not. Much of the gorgeous West African work (see section M) is done on a treadle machine with straight stitches only. However, a zigzag machine is very useful. If you do not have one, check with your local adult education department or high school home economics department to see if their machines are available for public use.

Scissors Cutting paper dulls scissors, so keep separate pairs for paper and for fabric. I have a special pair I hide from the family that is sharp to the very point and perfect for reverse appliqué.

Supplies (clockwise from upper right): masking tape, magnifier, felt-tipped pens, pincushion, scissors, needle threader, assorted threads, flexible ruler, French curve, X-acto knife, compass, right angle, colored papers, clear ruler, atlas, spray glue, rubber cement

Art Supplies

Your work will be much easier with proper supplies. The next time someone asks what you want for your birthday, whip out this list:

☐ a package of construction paper in bright colors (origami paper works well)

☐ pads of graph/tracing paper in 8½" × 11" and 11" × 17"; quarter-inch grid is useful for many projects in this book

☐ a roll of 1"-wide masking tape

☐ a can of spray adhesive or pattern spray; or a bottle of rubber cement

☐ a see-through ruler

☐ a set of felt-tipped pens in many colors

☐ a staple gun—for stretching fabrics on stretcher bars

☐ a right-angle triangle for squaring fabric on a frame and for marking 45° angles in mitering

☐ an inexpensive compass

☐ a French curve for making smooth curves (or a flexible ruler)

☐ an X-acto knife for easy cutting of leather, matboard, acetate, etc.

☐ an opaque projector (the height of luxury, but useful!)

Suggest to your gift-giver that some of these are more easily found in art supply stores than in yard-goods or needlework stores.

Miscellaneous Supplies

☐ Very soon after piercing my finger to the bone, I learned to love a thimble.

☐ For people who have less than 20-20 vision, a magnifier with a light is handy. However, do not set up the magnifier where the sun can reach it. There is an embarrassed woman on the East Coast who unwittingly started a fire, Girl Scout-style, on her dining room table.

☐ An atlas at hand makes the country you're studying more real. Look up your long-distance needlework friends.

TRANSFERRING DESIGNS

If the work is not counted thread, it is often necessary to transfer designs to your backing material before you begin. Sometimes this takes two steps: (1) Enlarge or reduce the design to the size you want, then (2) transfer the design.

Often you will want to enlarge a small design into something bigger or reduce one from something larger, so it is useful to know how to scale a design up or down. Fortunately there is a technique that lets you do this, even if you can't draw for beans.

The patterns in this book are all shown smaller than the actual project. They have a square grid placed over them to help you. On your own, you can achieve the same effect by laying ¼" (6mm) graph paper over a design and tracing the design onto it. Decide how much bigger you want the design—twice the size? three times?

Number and letter the squares as shown. Now take a fresh sheet of ¼" (6mm) graph paper and a ruler and rule off new squares. For example, if you want your new design twice as big, rule off every other line, both horizontally and vertically. If you want your finished design three times the size, rule off every third line. You will now have squares that are twice or three times the size of your original squares. Number and letter these new squares in exactly the same order as you did the original design. Start with square 1A and draw in the larger square whatever you see in the smaller square. Do this for each square . . . and surprise! your design is enlarged.

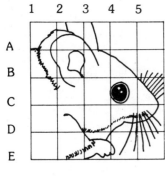

Original Cartoon

Enlarging and reducing a design

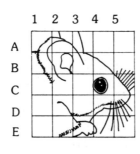

Reduced Cartoon

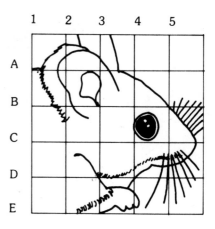

Enlarged Cartoon

Now you can use one of the following transfer methods to place your design on the material you've chosen.

There are at least six good methods to transfer designs onto fabric for embroidery, each dependent on the kind of fabric you've chosen or the type of work. These methods work when the design is already the exact size you want, ready to be transferred to your material.

Before we delve into the ways you can transfer designs to your material, we should decide how much of the design to transfer. Here, as is often the case, the rule is "least is best." In general, only the main lines or curves of your design need to be sketched in. At best, only the outlines of large, filled-in areas need to be put onto the transferred design.

The old, venerable name for such a line drawing is "cartoon." Long before the Saturday morning TV cartoons, the great painters of the Italian Renaissance were using cartoons to put their preliminary sketches for frescoes upon walls. We'll bow to tradition, even though the name "cartoon" now has an added connotation of fun—come to think of it, even the more modern use of "cartoon" fits what we're doing. In the remainder of this book, whenever we talk about a non-counted thread design, we'll assume that you can reduce your design to cartoon form.

From Allesandro Paganino, Il Burato, 1527: methods of transfer are not new—(from left) a medieval light table, tracing over a candle; tracing at a window; (right) pricking a design for pouncing.

In this book there are cartoons for every project requiring one. If you own this book, make copious notes on the colors to use, type of stitches, and so forth, directly on the cartoon. Refer to the notes as you work.

Onward, to methods of transferring designs.

1. My favorite is to lay a piece of tracing or tissue paper over the cartoon and to copy it with a black felt-tip pen. I often use the wrong side of outdated or extra tissue paper from clothing patterns, ignoring any print on the tissue. Wait a minute for the ink of the felt-tip pen to dry, so it won't smudge your fabric, then tape the fabric over the tissue paper to a window (during the day—what you're doing is using a makeshift light table). Tape the fabric over the tissue, centering the design, and trace the design onto the fabric with pencil or tailor's chalk. *Caution:* If you know the design line will not be completely covered by the thread, don't use an ordinary pencil for tracing the design as it does not always wash out. Use a colored washable pencil instead. You could also use a fine brush and blue watercolor, taking care not to mix too runny a mixture. On dark material I use a white pencil and on light material, a blue one. This method of tracing works on a surprising number of fabrics—from the most transparent fabric through medium-weight cottons with even surfaces. It does not work well on linen and textured fabrics.

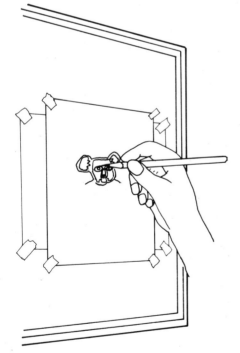

Tracing at the window

2. Another way to transfer designs that is particularly suited to the sewing machine is to copy the cartoon onto a piece of typing paper and then sew along the lines with an unthreaded machine, using a size 9 (60) sewing machine needle so that the holes in the paper are not too big. Pin or cellotape the paper to your fabric, centering the design wherever you want it, and gently rub pounce powder (similar to resin powder and available at needlework stores; or see supply list) over the lines of holes. I use a rolled-up pad of felt to apply the pounce to the fabric, gently rolling it into the holes of the typing paper and taking care not to put too much powder into the design at once. Pull up one corner of the typing paper from time to time to check whether enough pounce has gone through holes to mark your design sufficiently. Then carefully lift off the taped paper and lightly blow off the surplus pounce. If you try to brush it off, the pounce will smudge the fabric. This method works well on all fabric except the heavily textured and is especially useful for transferring repeat patterns. A clever variation of this method, minus the powder, is used in project B, Romanian embroidered yoke.

3. To transfer a design with dressmaker's carbon paper, available in any fabric store, tape your fabric to a hard surface, like a glass-topped desk or a Formica kitchen counter. Trace the cartoon onto tissue or tracing paper and center it on the fabric, weighting down the top edge with anything handy and heavy (scissors, paper weights, clean flower pots). Carefully slip a piece of dressmaker's carbon paper—don't use typing carbon paper because it smudges—between the tracing and the fabric, and then anchor the bottom edges of the tracing paper over it. Trace the design with an empty ball-point pen or the handle end of a letter opener. You have to push hard to produce a decent line on the fabric, but not so hard as to tear the tissue paper.

4. Transfer pencils are now available in needlework stores (see Another Mail-Order Supply List), taking some of the fuss out of transferring the design. Lay the tissue or tracing paper over the cartoon and copy with a felt-tipped pen. Let the ink dry and then turn the tissue paper over and retrace the design on the wrong side with the transfer pencil. Now lay the tissue paper on top of the fabric, the transfer pencil side against the fabric, and pin it carefully in place. Use an iron as hot as your fabric permits. Since the transfer lines sometimes rub off later as you work, as soon as the transfer cools I like to baste the main design as a safety precaution. Be sure to test the pencil on a piece of scrap fabric—red pencils sometimes run in washing.

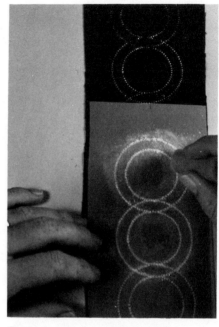

Prick the clear acetate with the sewing machine, then press pounce powder (talcum powder, cornstarch, powdered charcoal, or here, Dr. Scholl's Foot Powder) through the holes with a rolled-up pad of felt. Then connect the dots with a white pencil.

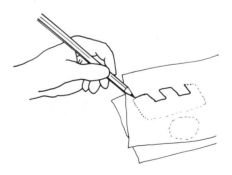

Trace the cartoon with a transfer pencil; (Letters must be traced backwards.)

25

Iron face-down onto fabric.

5. If you can get to a photocopy machine, you can save yourself a lot of time, especially on projects that are symmetrical around a center line. Photocopy two copies of the half-cartoons from the book, and flip one over; when placed so that the center lines overlap, the halves will form the full cartoon. This process is much easier if you can have the photocopies made on vellum, which is as transparent as tracing paper—check local drafting services for vellum. Often you can stitch right through the photocopy, as in section M, Africa.

6. All the methods above are greatly simplified by the use of an opaque projector. There are several inexpensive ones on the market but a larger, expensive model (still under $100) is well worth the money if you do a lot of stitching. If you belong to a local embroidery guild (see Resources), you may be able to buy the projector cooperatively. Otherwise, talk a local shopowner into buying one for rental use in the store.

WORKING OUR DESIGNS

Our cartoons are color- and stitch-coded and are on graphs for easy enlarging. (An arrow points to both the horizontal and vertical centers whenever possible.)

For all free embroidery you will transfer the cartoons to your fabric in one of the ways listed earlier. For the counted-thread designs, you must learn to read a graph, which is not difficult. Generally, each drawn line on the graph represents one complete stitch. The holes on the graph paper represent the holes of the fabric and the lines of the graph paper represent threads of the fabric. There are exceptions, though, so in the Project Pointers of graphed projects you'll find an explanation of how to read its graph.

To prevent mistakes such as misreading the graph, I strongly recommend that you practice each new technique on a doodle cloth, which is a small rectangle (say 5″ × 3″) of the fabric you are working on. I like to pin my doodle cloths to the page opposite the cartoon for later reference. Subject your doodle cloth to whatever wetness the final article will suffer—such as wetting waste canvas, pressing with a wet press cloth, washing in a machine, and so on. It's better to have threads run on a doodle cloth than on the actual work.

MISCELLANEOUS WORKING TIPS

☐ When using a hoop, imagine it to be a clock. If you're right-handed, keep the screw of the hoop at 10 o'clock; if left-handed, at 2 o'clock. This will minimize the thread macraméing itself around the screw with every stitch.

☐ Also when using a hoop, frame, or stretcher bars, keep your smarter hand underneath.

☐ If you're working with lots of colors, keep one needle threaded with each color so you don't have to thread and unthread the same needle.

☐ If you own this book, it helps to decode a graph by coloring in each section with felt-tipped pens as you are ready to stitch with that color thread.

☐ Be sure to wash your hands before working on light fabrics. The oil on your fingertips attracts dirt. If you are afraid that the fabric or threads will be soiled as you embroider, place tissue paper over the work before you mount it in the hoop or frame. Then tear away the section of tissue paper covering where you want to work.

☐ If blood from a pricked finger soils the fabric, quickly chew some white sewing thread and blot the spot with the thread. Apparently your saliva cleans up your blood. Better yet, wear a thimble on one hand and keep Band-Aids in your work box.

☐ An iron is a handy marking tool. Keep one set up near your work area. Use it to mark the center of the fabric by pressing in the center folds, to mark a long line for stitching, and to divide your fabric into any sections.

☐ Mistakes—everyone makes them. Cut an unwanted thread carefully from the back, and, using a blunt needle, remove stitches. They say we learn from our mistakes, but "they" must not embroider. Work slowly so you don't make them. It hurts to rip five hours of work in five minutes.

☐ Your attitude while stitching definitely affects your work. In many cultures a person is not allowed to embroider unless (s)he feels calm and loving. Otherwise bad spirits enter the work. Approach your own work with goodwill, and it seems to give it back to you. As I stitch I like to listen to stories and plays on records from the public library. One of my friends listens to the local public broadcasting station; another is learning a language while he stitches; yet another good friend rents taped books that she listens to more than once.

☐ Some of these designs are more portable than others. I like to keep projects appropriate for a long car or plane trip near the door

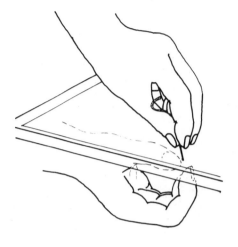

Keep your "smart" hand under the frame.

in a bag that I can easily grab on my way out. In modern life we seem to spend hours a day waiting; embroidery makes it bearable.

☐ Folk art throughout history has usually been anonymous, to the frustration of collectors and descendants. Do sign and date all your work. You can develop a logo for your work or a stitch signature, as is done in Mexico, rather than embroider your entire name. Just be sure that somewhere it's recorded what your logo is and what it means.

☐ Also please keep a written and visual record of everything you stitch. Your children and future historians will love you for it. I have a log (really a small 15¢ notebook) similar to this:

ITEM	DIMENSIONS	ORIGINAL?	MATERIALS	TECH-NIQUE	STITCHES	LOCATION	PHOTO NUMBER AND LOCATION	COMMENTS (awards, etc.)
purse	14″ × 21″	purchased	3-ply wool on #14 cotton canvas	canvas work	basket-weave	in use	slide file #15	two different dye lots of same orange fading into different colors—shown in PSG show, date

It is really inspiring to see how much you've accomplished over the years, and very easy to forget without a log.

☐ In taking pictures, either snapshot or slide, get as close as your camera will permit. People are interested in your embroidery, not the chair it's sitting on. If you can, photograph outside before 10 A.M. and after 4 P.M. in the shade of a (preferably) white building. If your house is blue polka-dot, tape up some white fabric or paper so the reflections on your work will not affect its color.

☐ As long as you're taking pictures, why not have a quantity of them made of one project to mount on heavy paper as greeting cards for the holiday season? (See Section K, Hardanger greeting card.)

PRESSING, BLOCKING, AND MITERING

Every piece of embroidery needs to be blocked, whether it was worked on a frame or not. I like to put the work face down on a clean folded towel, put a moist press-cloth over the work, and *press* (not iron) the work with an iron heated to a temperature appropriate to the materials used (details in sections on natural fabrics). Pressing means lifting the iron from place to place; ironing means sliding the iron from one place to another.

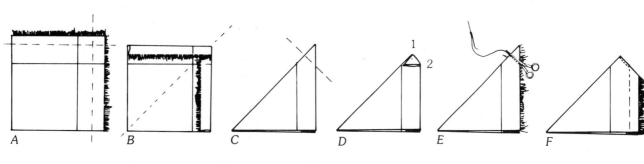

CARING FOR EMBROIDERY

Before washing, determine what kinds of threads were used in the embroidery, fabric backing, trim, and fastenings. More than one pillow has been ruined by the color of a cheap zipper running. If all components are washable, fill a bowl with warm water and soap flakes. Let the work soak no more than ten minutes (after that, the dirt in the water begins to reenter the fabric). Squeeze gently—don't wring the work—and lift to a bowl of clean warm water. While the embroidery soaks, throw the water from the first bowl on your houseplants. A final rinse in cool water is optional. Wool items should be washed in cold water with soap made especially for it; silk should be dry-cleaned. Roll the wet item in a towel and press out the excess water. Then spread on a dry towel away from sun and heaters until dry. Press face-down into a folded towel.

COLLECTING ETHNIC EMBROIDERY

There is tremendous interest in this country in building a good embroidery collection. By a combination of first-hand travel, mail order, import, and antique stores, you can collect a fair pile. Like quilts, embroidery looks as good on the wall as in use, so display your collection for everyone's enjoyment.

Again, the garage sale is often a source of embroidery. While I was photographing in the University of California/Berkeley Textile Collection in the Visual Design Department, a man came in with the story of a friend who had recently bought a tapestry at a garage sale for $3.50. She merely thought the design was pretty. When she took it to an antique dealer's for cleaning and framing, he casually mentioned that the tapestry was worth $32,000.

Many people collect embroidery while traveling abroad. Don't forget your own country, though. Lots of beautiful work is done by artists and craftspeople in your own territory. It would be a shame to let our needlework culture go down the drain for lack of financial patronage, while we support whole needle-wielding villages abroad.

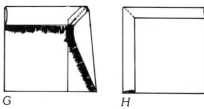

A. Mark a line about 1″ in from raw edges by pulling a thread each way.

B. Turn raw edges in ¼″ to top-side and press.

C. Fold folded edges, right sides together.

D. Fold point to line you marked in A. Press.

E. Open up entire fabric flat, including raw edges. Refold on diagonal line you made in C. Sew from 1 to 2 on the diagonal line you made in D (1 is ¼″ from the raw edge, on the line you marked in B).

F. Trim ⅛″ from the sewn line, extending it to the raw edges.

G. Press the seam open and flip the mitered corner to the underside of the fabric.

H. Turn under the ¼″ edges and hem.

part one 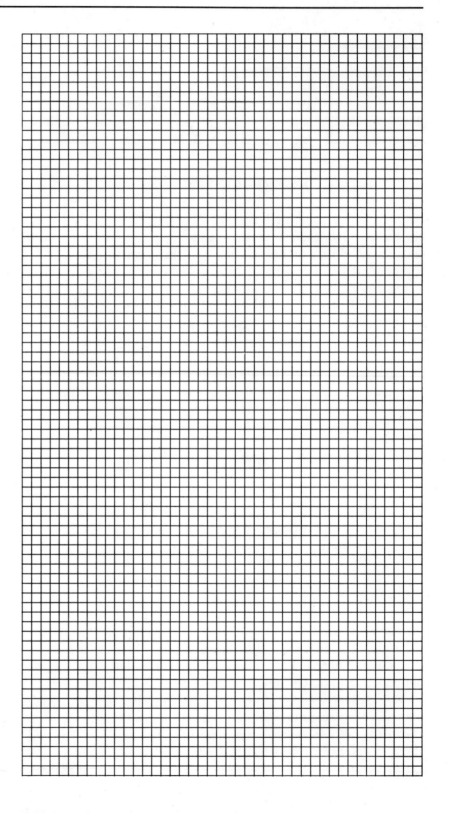 SKINS

Wearing the skins of animals around them was prehistoric people's sensible solution to cold and rain. After all, the pelts were at hand anytime the hunter brought home meat, and the skins required no particular preparation except rubbing or beating into a flexible form. The skin felt good, and it was warm without being suffocating.

At first thorns or bone splinters were probably used to connect skin to skin. Fortunately for us, thorns do not hold pelts together well—two chases after a jackrabbit and one flight from a saber-toothed tiger would convince a prehistoric person that there had to be a better way. First came simple lacing together of the skins with sinew or animal hair. Embroidery and surface decoration followed soon after.

The properties of leather have led to imaginative uses in cultures throughout history. Its strength attracted the Vikings, who made leather sails for their warships. Its protective qualities were used by the legions of Rome, who made body shields from it. Musical instruments, toys like leather shadow puppets, games like chess and leather checkers—the uses of leather are truly unlimited.

Leather is technically the tanned or treated covering of any creature that biologically has skin, including snakes, birds, and mammals. Today, we tend to use the covering of large domestic animals such as sheep and cows, rather than the skins of our precious wild animals.

We also tend to be more interested in the leather itself than the fur, so what we use for clothing today generally comes from animals with short hair. This hair is removed before the skin is tanned.

Tanning was originally done with vegetable or bark matter (tannin), but since 1800 chromium sulfate has generally been used as the tanning agent (called chrome tanning). The purpose of tanning is to transform the leather into something that won't rot.

There are as many kinds of leather as there are animals. Therefore it would be as meaningless to say, "Buy some leather to make a purse," as to say, "Buy some fabric for a jacket"—net, felt, silk, velvet?

Some kinds of leather and their uses are listed:

Leather	*Uses*
buckskin	gloves, American Indian garments
calfskin	shoes, purses, luggage
cowskin	wide variety of uses and names, depending on how it's treated and its thickness—e.g., "latigo" is cowhide tanned in vegetable oil

goatskin	shoes, "Moroccan leather," kid cushions, chamois
pigskin	used in gloves, undersoles, footballs
sheepskin	often called suede or chamois, used for garments

Two terms refer to which side of the leather was rained on when it still covered the animal. *Grain side* refers to the outer side from which hair was removed, leaving a slight texture from exposed pores; this side can be polished to make it shiny, or buffed for a matte appearance. *Flesh side* indicates the underside of the leather closest to the bones; when it is buffed and dyed, it is a *suede*.

Where to buy leather? If you live in a city, look in the telephone yellow pages under "Leather," "Tanners," "Arts and Crafts Supplies," or "Shoe Findings and Suppliers." Also, large fabric stores often carry garment leather, which is what we used for project B, Romanian embroidered yoke.

If you live out of town your leather sources (other than those munching in the barnyard) may be reached by mail (see supply list). Don't forget secondhand stores, garage sales, and your own attic as sources of leather. Old boots make fine noses for stuffed koala bears; old purses can be cut down into wallets, picture frames, and key rings.

SEWING ON LEATHER

Sewing on leather by machine is not difficult with the help of either a wing needle or a leather-point needle, which is shaped like a wedge. The size of the needle depends on the thickness of the leather; ask your fabric store owner to help you. If you have a roller presser foot for your machine, use it. Otherwise place tissue paper between the leather and the needle plate. The tissue paper will protect the leather from being scratched by the feed dogs and moves the leather through without sticking or slipping. After sewing, the tissue is easily torn off.

The thread used should be strong, such as silk buttonhole twist, cotton-covered polyester, or heavy carpet thread (remember to use a larger-eyed machine needle).

Machine stitches too close together will rip light-weight leather, so set your machine for 6 to 10 stitches/inch. Do not backstitch to start and end threads; tie off the ends by hand.

Sewing on leather by hand is far easier if you let your sewing machine help you get started. Use a wing needle to transfer your design to the leather. The holes punched in the leather this way allow you to use an ordinary tapestry needle and such otherwise difficult threads as embroidery wool directly on leather (see project B).

Seams and darts can be pressed with a low iron setting. Do not use steam, and do use a press cloth or brown paper between the leather and the iron. Because you are working with a bulky fabric, you might want to use a leatherworker's trick for flattening seams. Put rubber cement between each side of the seam and the underside of the garment. Pound the underside of the seam lightly with a mallet or the spine of a fat book.

CARE OF LEATHER

Wearable leather is best cared for by a cleaning establishment familiar with its handling. Ordinary steam cleaning streaks and destroys leather color. If you wear your leather garment often, have it cleaned at least once a year, if not more often.

Garments, such as in project B, Romanian embroidered yoke, which are combinations of leather and a woven or knit fabric should always be dry-cleaned. For small items made of suede there are sprays that lift off dirt. Items made of smooth leather can be cleaned with a damp sponge or saddle soap, as long as the leather is not painted with a water-base paint or ink.

Do not fold leather—the crease lines will not come out. Instead, roll it around a mailing tube or butcher paper if you cannot hang it up. Before working, I hung the leather used for project B from a two-clip skirt hanger.

Since leather is subject to mildew, do not store it in warm, damp places.

Many rain-proofing preparations exist for leather. If there is no leather-supply store near you, try the closest shoe-repair store; lacking that, you can try a shoe store. Of course, your leather should be treated and allowed to dry before you stitch on it.

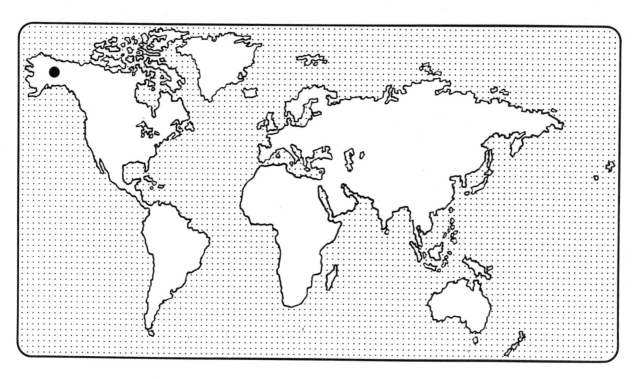

ESKIMO

The average temperatures above the Arctic circle are 50°F in the summer and −10°F in the winter. Because of this overwhelming element, cold, the Eskimo must be in movement almost constantly, both to keep warm and to find food and fuel. That Eskimo clothing has any decoration on it at all is a tribute to humanity's innate need to bring beauty to environment.

Eskimo decoration brings fine art to fur tailoring. By mixing fur textures and purposely altering some by shearing, the Eskimo creates a variety of color and pattern without sacrificing warmth.

To provide the greatest protection from cold, clothing is layered, and two parkas are worn. The inner parka is worn fur-side in over trousers, boots, socks, and mittens. Those who live on the seacoast use skins for boats and waterproof boots, while farther south snowshoes and moccasins are made of available leathers.

If you want to understand the very basics in embroidery and appliqué, study and interpret for yourself the three major ways Eskimos embellish their clothing:

1. Between seams—from a simple overcast stitch to hold skins together come cross stitch and buttonhole stitch. By running red worsted thread in and out of the seam and later clipping it, the Eskimo embroiderer creates a simple emphasis of design shapes.

2. By replacement of a garment section with a decorative unit—such as constructing a fur patchwork unit and inserting it, say, in the yoke.

3. By adding decorative margins at the hem, wrist, or hood—for example, adding different colored bands of leather or more checkerboard squares of fur.

If you employ only these three ways to decorate your clothing, your wardrobe will have a unique and varied appearance.

The Eskimos use simple embroidery stitches to hold carved ivory pendants onto the bottom of a parka. These pendants are attractive and they weight the garment so it won't blow up in a wind (the heavy fringe of the American Indians does the same thing)—but best of all, they make a wonderful rattling music as a person walks.

Eskimo parka with a variety of furs and bands of leather. The dark dots on the leather are tufts of red wool running stitch, clipped as shown on page 37. Collection of the Lowie Museum of Anthropology, University of California, Berkeley.

WORKING PROCESS:
Patchwork Wallet *See also color plate 4*

In constructing a simple patchwork wallet that salutes the Eskimo skill with furs, we call on an all-American technique: Seminole Indian patchwork. This technique is so useful to have in your repertoire that even if you don't plan to make the wallet, it's worth reading the directions so you can use the technique elsewhere.

Project Pointers

¼″ seam allowance everywhere—fake fur often sheds where you cut it, so work where a mess doesn't matter, and keep a wastebasket near.

Make sure the nap is running the same way on adjacent pieces.

Trim excess fur from the seam allowances before stitching.

Measure and cut accurately.

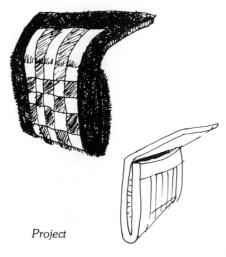

Project

YOU WILL NEED

8″ × 9½″ rectangle dark knit-backed fake fur
11½″ × 4½″ rectangle each, light and medium knit-backed fake fur
8½″ × 13½″ lining
1 strand, red Persian wool
scissors, sewing machine

1. To construct the center checkerboard area, cut 3 strips each of your light and medium furs 11½″ × 1½″. With your scissors trim the excess fur off the ¼″ seam allowance all around each strip. Sew by hand or machine the long edges of four strips to each other, alternating medium and light strips. Make sure the nap runs the same way.

2. Cut off 8½″ of the long striped fabric you constructed in step 1. These cuts must all be exact and at right angles so mark the fur on its knit back with a pencil or felt-tipped pen. Sew the remaining light fur strip to this 8½″ piece next to the medium strip. Cut off the excess light strip.

Cartoon

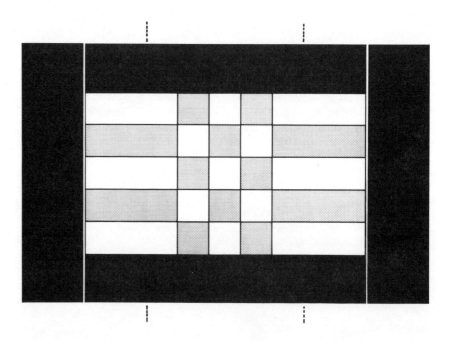

3. Make two cuts across the 8½″ piece you just constructed: one 1½″ from an end and the other cutting what remains in half so each is 3½″ long.

4. Sew the remaining medium strip to the light side of the 3″ piece you constructed in steps 1 and 2.

5. Cut 3″ piece from step 4 in half into two 1½″ pieces.

6. Now lay out the checkerboard on your sewing table, following the cartoon. Make sure the nap is all running in one direction. Carefully sew each section to its neighbor, right sides together, pinning the seams that touch together.

7. Cut the dark rectangle into two 9½″ × 2½″ strips and two 8½″ × 2½″ strips. Sew the two 2″ × 9½″ dark fur pieces to either side of the long checkerboard.

8. Sew the remaining two dark pieces across the ends of the wallet.

9. Thread one strand of red Persian wool into a tapestry needle. Before you sew long running stitches all around the perimeter of the checkerboard, anchor the thread on the back with several backstitches in the dark seam allowance. Hold the seam open on the back with your left hand as you take long running stitches (at least ¼″) right through the seam. When you are done, cut the running stitches on the top in half. The results are funny little tufts of red hiding in the fur—a humorous Eskimo touch.

10. Lay the lining piece of the fur, right sides together, and stitch all around, leaving an opening for turning. Clip corners, turn, and close opening with a ladder stitch.

11. Turn up 4″ as shown above and slipstitch the sides together to make an envelope purse.

ADDITIONAL IDEAS

1. Use this design for a dollhouse rug (see section R, Uzbek embroidery dollhouse rug).
2. Do you have a child, grandchild, or young friend who is learning to read? For a special fuzzy reading rug, enlarge this design so that every inch on the cartoon equals 6″.
3. Think of the many ways you can use the Seminole checkerboard technique: borders for pillows, tablecloths, panel replacements for wearables, placemats, hangings. Experiment with two, three, and more colors for some surprising effects.

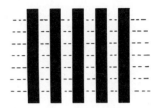

Construct a long rectangle of light and medium fur. Then slice it off as needed and stagger the slices to produce a checkerboard.

Running stitches in the seams are cut on top.

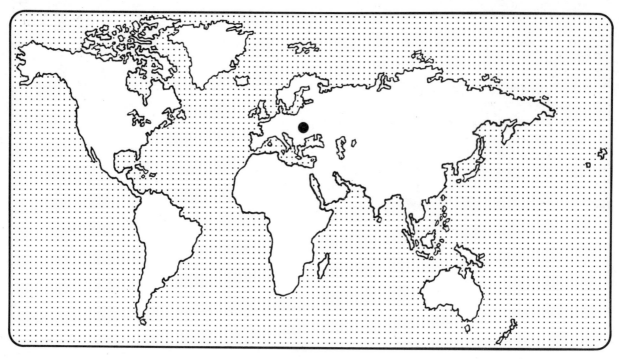

ROMANIA

One feature travelers through Romania immediately notice is the abundance of brightly embroidered sheepskin coats.

The manufacture of these fleece-lined leather coats is a trade, not a home art, and the coats are expensive. Perhaps the bright patches of wool embroidery recall summer's flowers and hot sun in the midst of Romania's hard winters. (When it rains, the people turn the coats inside out so the embroidery will be protected.) Besides flowers, there are embroidered rosettes and solar symbols that are the sign of an ancient agricultural tradition of planting by the stars.

Romania has been in the pathway of major invasions throughout history. As a result the people became accustomed to fleeing for their lives. Among other things, this encouraged embroidery on portable objects like clothing (when you're off to the hills, you take a coat, not an embroidered tea tray).

The Romans, who last occupied the land from 106–271 A.D., were among the most influential invaders. This link shows up in embroidery on blouse sleeves. Instead of the usual decoration on the cuff and perhaps a band down the sleeve, the Romanians embroider in a spiral band up the sleeve, reminiscent of Roman designs on columns.

The people use all the bright colors in their needlework but are especially fond of reds in all shades. One favorite is a yellowish-red similar to an overripe wild cherry; it is known in Romania as "rotten cherry red."

These colors used to be naturally dyed, and just as Romanians planted by the stars, they harvested plant materials for natural dyes when the heavens and planets were all lined up correctly. Women were not allowed to do any dyeing unless they were happy and healthy and free from worry. (I've often been tempted to use this argument with housework: "I can't do the dishes this month because I'm worried about the sassafras harvest.")

We can all learn how to apply principles of pattern, color, and rhythm to our own work by studying Romanian dress. First of all, the main patterns are designed to be bold and colorful from a distance. These colors blend harmoniously with the usually white blouses and aprons. Second, the areas of pattern are not allowed to be surrounded by bare patches of backing. The same or a similar pattern will be worked delicately at regular intervals between major embroidered parts. This variety and fineness of work pleases the eye at close range. Finally, the needleworker would rather embroider a totally new design, no matter how difficult, than be forced to duplicate something already worked. Each time (s)he embroiders a traditional design, (s)he changes some colors or adds something to make it personal.

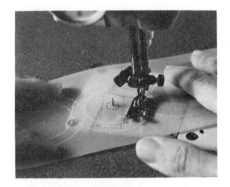

Making circles and parts of circles is easy with a thumbtack and an unthreaded sewing machine.

WORKING PROCESS:
Wool Embroidery on Leather (Yoke on Jacket of Woman's Suit)

In the larger towns where many different nationalities (Hungarians, Saxons, etc.) mingle, the sheepskin coat-makers cleverly use a little of everybody's art to please any taste. So do we; who can resist a rainbow?

Our method of marking a circle or part of a circle is another valuable skill worth learning, like the patchwork construction in the last project. Working with a wing needle and an unthreaded sewing machine makes marking the leather extremely easy and lets you stitch with wool yarn on the leather with a blunt tapestry needle. Since the holes will be pre-punched by machine, the actual stitching is nearly effortless. (For an exercise in frustration, try sewing on leather without pre-punching.)

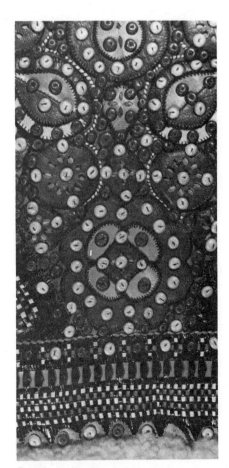

Detail from Romanian leather applique coat. Photo courtesy the Museum of New Mexico.

Project photo

Project Pointers

Use thin rubber cement, not thick, when making the leather
  sandwich.
Don't fold leather while it's waiting to be embroidered.

YOU WILL NEED

pattern for woman's jacket with yoke (or use a ready-made jacket if
  you're willing to remove the yoke for working)
1 strand each, 3-ply Persian wool: gold, lemon yellow, orange,
  tangerine, pink, magenta, rose, violet, light violet, blue, sky blue,
  turquoise, green, chartreuse
1 skein each: scarlet and yellow
sewing machine (preferably with a zigzag)
1 sewing machine wing needle (or a sewing machine leather needle)
enough garment leather to fit your yoke
fabric for the rest of the jacket
tapestry needle, scissors, ruler, pencil, tape, 1 thumbtack
2 large pieces of smooth typing-weight paper (graph paper is ideal)
spray adhesive or rubber cement
doodle cloth

1. Cut the yoke out of the leather.

2. Lay the yoke pattern on one of the large pieces of graph paper.
Trace around it. You will no longer need the tissue yoke pattern.

3. On the graph paper draw a straight line ¾″ from the bottom edge
of yoke. You will use this line to set up the placement of the rainbows. There are two rows of rainbows; each row consists of three
arches per rainbow. Draw another line parallel to the first and ⅝″
above it.

4. Starting ¼″ in from the left on the bottom line, mark every 2″
across the line. These will be the centers of the rainbows. On the
line above the bottom line, mark every 2″ starting 1¼″ from the left
edge and making sure the centers of the second rows are 1″ on
either side of the centers on the first row. You only need trace from
the cartoon the upper line of red stitching and the two yellow circles
with their centers.

5. Apply a coat of spray adhesive or *thin* rubber cement (thick will give you problems) to the other sheet of graph paper. Let it dry for a few minutes until sticky. Lay the wrong side of the leather yoke on the sticky paper.

6. Spray the wrong side of the marked graph paper, as in step 5. Let dry until sticky. Place on the right side of the leather (it won't hurt it), lining up the outline of the yoke pattern with the yoke. Smooth the papers so they'll stick to the yoke. Trim off the excess paper. These papers keep the leather from buckling as you mark it on the machine.

7. Put the wing needle in the machine, unthreaded. Turn the hand wheel and pierce your leather sandwich (paper-leather-paper) in the centers of all the rainbows.

8. Now mark the stitching lines on the arches, but first please set up a 3″ × 5″ doodle cloth identical to the leather sandwich. Measure 1″ to the left of the hole in your needle plate. Put the sticker of a thumbtack upside-down on the 1″. Tape it in place, letting the tack pierce the tape. Set your machine for its widest zigzag and for a short stitch length. Experiment on the doodle cloth until you find a stitch length with the holes close together without ripping the leather.

9. Now mark the actual yoke. Starting at the left side of the yoke on the bottom line put the center of the first rainbow on the tack. This first rainbow is incomplete because it falls at the edge of the yoke.

Wing needle

The order in which you pre-punch your holes in the leather

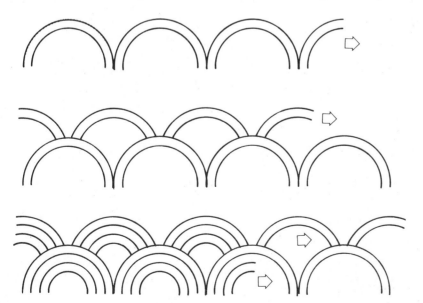

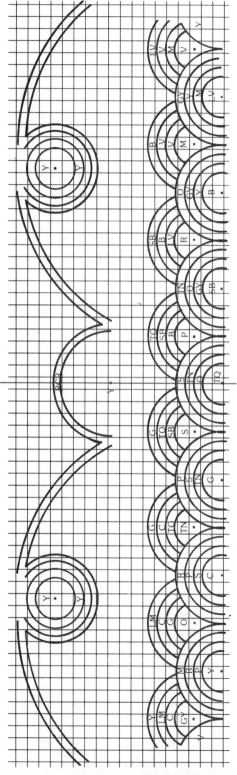

Begin with the needle at the right of its swing. Stitch with the unthreaded sewing needle until you reach the bottom line.

10. Move the sandwich over to the next rainbow, sticking the center of the rainbow on the tack. Begin the needle on the right of its swing, in or as near as possible to the hole on the bottom line of the first rainbow. Mark all the rainbows on the first and second rows in this manner.

11. Now move the tack so it is ⅝" from the needle hole. Mark the inner arch of each rainbow on the first and second rows.

12. Stitch with the unthreaded machine along the upper line of stitching, which you copied from the cartoon. Use the ⅝" tack method for the two yellow circles (it's easiest).

13. Carefully peel off the two layers of paper. Now it is very easy to satin stitch with the tapestry needle and the Persian wool in colors as shown on the cartoon. In fact Tony worked most of the yoke one night when he couldn't sleep from an ear infection. Begin and end threads by weaving them in on the back.

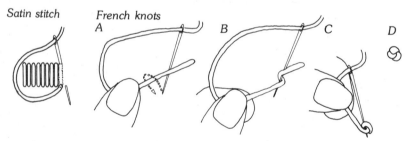

Satin stitch *French knots*

14. Do French knots in the centers of all the rainbows.

15. Construct the rest of the garment, following your pattern instructions. You can easily make leather cuffs, using a portion of the rainbow color progression on each cuff. (Don't forget to change the wing needle for a regular needle when sewing.)

Color Code

RCH = Rotten Cherry Red
S = Scarlet
TN = Tangerine
O = Orange
GY = Gold-Yellow
LM = Lemon
C = Chartreuse
G = Green

TQ = Turquoise
SB = Sky Blue
LV = Light Violet (Lavender)
V = Violet
M = Magneta
R = Rose
P = Pink

1 square = ¼"

ADDITIONAL IDEAS

1. Use leftover garment leather to make a key ring. Mark two pieces of leather with one rainbow and stitch right through both layers. Overcast the edges with rotten-cherry red.
2. Combine the wallet pattern from section A, Eskimo patchwork wallet, with the rainbow design to make a leather gift for a friend.
3. Make leather buttons with one French knot on each, all in different colors.

SUPPLIES AND BIBLIOGRAPHY—SKINS

Dewey Decimal library call numbers given in parentheses when known

Leather

Krohn, Margaret B., and Schweoke, Phyllis W. *How to Sew Leather, Suede, Fur.* New York: Bruce, 1966, 1970. $6.95 (646S).

Perry, Patricia, ed. *From Vogue Patterns, Everything About Sewing Leather and Leather-Like Fabrics.* New York: Butterick, 1971. $1.50.

Things to Do With Leather. Menlo Park, CA: Sunset Books, Lane Publishing, 1973. $1.95 (q745.535).

American Tanners Association, 411 Fifth Ave., New York, NY 10016.

Berman Leathercraft, 145–147 South St., Boston, MA 02111—color catalog, $1, very complete.

The Dead Cow, 1040 River St., Santa Cruz, CA 95050—free price list.

The Leather Works, 628 Emerson St., Palo Alto, CA 94301—free catalog.

Cape by K. Lee Manuel, laced and painted leather, painted feathers and feathers painted on.

Eskimos

Burnford, Sheila. *One Woman's Arctic.* Boston: Little, Brown, 1972. $7.95 (970.4B).

Speck, Frank G. *"Eskimo Jacket Ornaments." American Antiquity* vol. 5, January 1940.

Romania

Harkness, Dorothy Norris. "Romania Embroidery, A Dying Folk Art." *The Bulletin of the Needle and Bobbin Club,* vol. 43, 1957.

part two 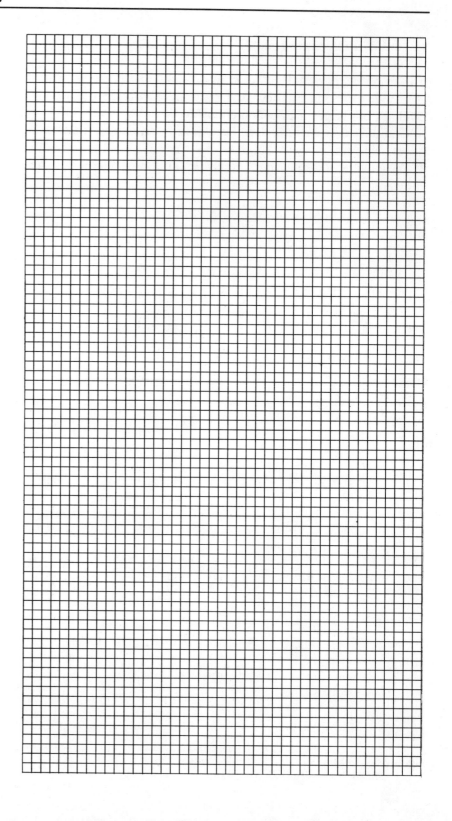 LINEN

I magine: One cold, dry winter day you get up very early to hike beside the lake outside your town. No one is around when you arrive, except some loud bluejays and a cardinal. You walk down the frozen mud banks of the lake, which are exposed more than usual because the waters have receded so much. Your eyes look across the lake . . . and look again. There, sticking out of the lake bottom are strange shacklike houses perched on poles.

Most of the shacks are out of your reach, but you are able to peer into one. It is old, very old, with crude tools heaped in a corner. You begin to suspect that you've discovered something important, and you imagine a primitive society crouched around a fire. Reaching through the door you extract a watertight container decorated with chevrons and spirals. It takes some tugging and prying with your Army knife to force the lid open. There lies a shiny gray length of finely woven linen—is this the product of a primitive society?

Such an incident did occur during the extremely cold winter of 1853–1854 in Switzerland and northern Italy. Sticking out of the alpine lakes were the ancient homes of the Stone Age Lake Dwellers. Investigation uncovered woven and plaited fabrics of flax, bast (a strong, woody fiber), and wool. This proved that very early humanity had already learned the important skill of twisting threads together to make a continuous filament.

Simple weaving had existed long before this twisting or spinning, but the natural length of a fiber limited its use. People could imitate the natural world in simple weaving—baskets like the nests of birds, fishing nets like spider webs, small animal snares like wasp cones. But when (wo)man learned to lengthen fibers artificially, we became able to make clothes and shelter so that we could migrate to better places, and once there, we wanted to plant fields to grow more fiber. Humanity had changed from the Hunting Age to the Pastoral Age to the Agricultural Age.

The flax plant is the source of linen and Egypt is often called the home of linen, although the flax plant knew no national boundaries and also grew elsewhere. Nevertheless, the Egyptians believed flax was the first thing made by their gods for them. They developed the weaving of a linen so fine that a length of yardage could be pulled through a finger ring. To this day, we have not been able to duplicate so fine a weave.

The way different cultures viewed each other back then was as funny and biased as it is today. When linen first reached Greece through trade routes, the men of the mountains considered it effeminate. Mountains called for warm clothing—and that meant wool. Meanwhile, the Egyptians and the Chinese regarded people who wore wool and had beards as barbarians and bandits. A little later, the Turks thought the clean-shaven, silk-clad Chinese weak and unmasculine. In the same vein, Aristophanes reported that Grecian dowagers sneered at the filthy Egyptian habit of using a linen square as a handkerchief. The ladies said "No thank you!" and stuck to their own method, using a foxtail.

As linen moved out of Egypt into the western world, it was chosen both as an embroidery thread and as a backing (for its exquisite handling properties). It is easy to work with and very strong and durable (which is also why it survived until the Lake Dwellers discovery). Different cultures have explored its many variations. In Flanders, for example, linen fabric was altered by withdrawing threads in one direction and embroidering on the remaining exposed threads. This was the precursor of Flemish lace. In France, the most famous use of linen fabric is the Bayeux Tapestry, a long, embroidered scroll commemorating the Battle of Hastings.

Politics and textiles have been interwoven throughout history. In fact, I might have enjoyed history as a school subject more in my youth had it been told from the point of view of textiles rather than dates. For example, in 1685 the revocation of the Edict of Nantes, which had protected the civil and religious rights of the Huguenots, a Protestant minority, drove more than 600,000 textile workers from France to England and Ireland. This almost wrecked the entire textile industry of France, and has been called "one of the most flagrant blunders in the history of France." Later Ireland, with its French emigré textile workers, became a center for the linen industry because of pressure from English businessmen. They didn't want the English wool industry threatened by competition, so they "encouraged" Ireland to develop a linen, rather than wool trade. The famous Irish linen, one of many weights of linen fabric, was the result.

CARE OF LINEN

Care of linen fabric is easy: machine-wash it in hot water and dry at regular cycle, removing the garment when slightly damp. Don't bleach colored linens.

Iron at medium heat for finer linens, hot for more loosely woven.

If you scorch the fabric, dampen the scorched area and let the sun bleach it out. Keep the area damp until the tan disappears.

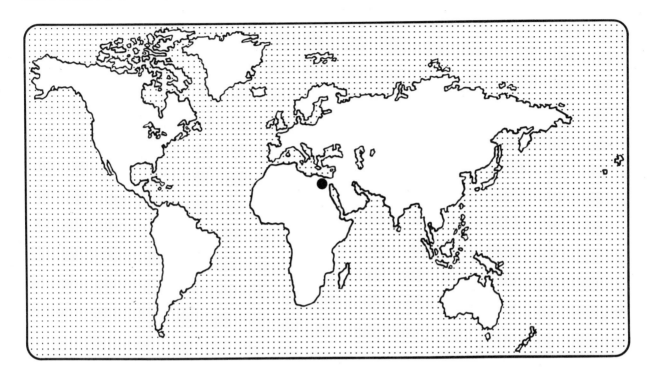

EGYPT

Egyptian art, whether painting, sculpture, or needlework, was shaped by 3000 years of an early, stable political system. Art was monumental and slow to change, using the same images time and again. The widely used lotus, for example, was a mystical symbol of the river Nile, the life-giving force that preserved humanity from the arid desert. Sir William Flinders Petrie, the great explorer of Egypt, said that the lotus motif spread so widely throughout the world that "some have seen in it the source of all ornament." He points to such descendants as the medieval French *fleur-de-lys*.

Both weaving and embroidery were favored by the Egyptian rulers, but in massive quantities. During the 31-year reign of Rameses III, 37,882 linen garments were given to the gods. A lesser ruler had an embroidered tent that took 50 artists nine years to work and was so huge it took 100 camels to carry it.

Yards of linen were also needed for the mummification of the dead. After an elaborate ritual for preservation involving many wrapped layers of linen, traditional designs were painted on the mummy. These same designs were painted on the ceiling of the tombs, carved on statues, and repeated in embroidery.

Appliqué was used both in early Egypt and after the time of Christ. Boats on the Nile had bold designs appliquéd on linen sails, probably to identify merchants to one another. Much later the Christians in Egypt, called Copts, embroidered fine tapestry medallions on linen tunics, until persecution by the Romans changed their technique. Lacking time for embroidery, they sewed bits of fabric in circle and square shapes to their robes, which was not only basic appliqué, but the beginnings of ecclesiastical vestments.

By examining Egyptian ornament and applying its principal categories to our own work, we can give great diversity to our needlework. These four categories can be used as an outline to examine the ornament of any culture, including our own.

1. Simple geometric ornament—lines, spirals, curves, squares, circles
2. Natural ornament—copying the world around us (flowers, animals, growth patterns)
3. Structural ornament that is dictated by building and manufacture—brickwork, tile patterns
4. Symbolic ornament—the lotus, water drops

Modern Egyptian appliqué, cotton on cotton, collection of Diana Leone.

WORKING PROCESS:
Appliqué on Soft Jewelry

In ancient Egypt linen was difficult to dye, so color was added by beadwork, jewels, flowers, and painting on fabric. We've combined this last technique with the memory of Queen Isis-em-Kheb's funeral canopy, which consisted of squares of gazelle hide of different colors appliquéd to linen. Adapting to today's materials, we've painted a soft collar of imitation suede and appliquéd it to linen.

Project Pointers

Use an unthreaded sewing machine and a wing needle to mark fabric for handstitching.

YOU WILL NEED

11″ × 14″ piece of cream-colored imitation suede
8″ × 13″ piece of turquoise imitation suede
½ yard light blue linen
½ yard each, interfacing and lining
textile paints*: rust (purchase, or mix by adding small amount of black to red) and blue
paint brush
1 skein each, #5 pearl cotton: black and white
2 tapestry needles, scissors
black sewing machine thread and sewing machine with wing or leather needle
20″ black narrow ribbon or braid
graph or tracing paper, typing-weight scrap paper
(optional): compass, spray adhesive, X-acto knife or razor blade, ruler

* Note: These same colors can be used in section V, Peru.

1. Blow up and transfer the cartoon to the graph paper. The easiest way is to use a compass, but a pencil with a string tied to it can also be used. Put an X on the center of the graph paper about 7″ from the top. This will match the X on the cartoon. One slice of the collar is shown actual size. Put the point of the compass on the slice's X and adjust the compass pencil to the same size radius as the outer

edge of the collar. Now without changing this radius, put the compass point on your graph paper X. Swing a complete circle. Do this for all the circular lines on the slice and you will have blown up the majority of the collar. Transfer the neck and back edges by the grid method.

2. Cut the collar out of the interfacing and try it on. Make any adjustments necessary and mark them on the graph paper. The collar should lie flat all around. It closes in back by tying, so it does not have to meet in back.

3. Cut the collar out of linen and lining fabric.

4. On a second piece of tracing or graph paper trace the outline of the turquoise imitation suede. Cut it out. The easiest way is to spray adhesive on the back of the tracing paper. Let it dry a few minutes till sticky. Then place it directly on the turquoise imitation suede and smooth it down. The adhesive will not affect the fabric. For a clean straight line, cut the imitation suede using the ruler and the X-acto knife or razor, putting an old magazine or newspaper under the fabric. Remove the tracing paper.

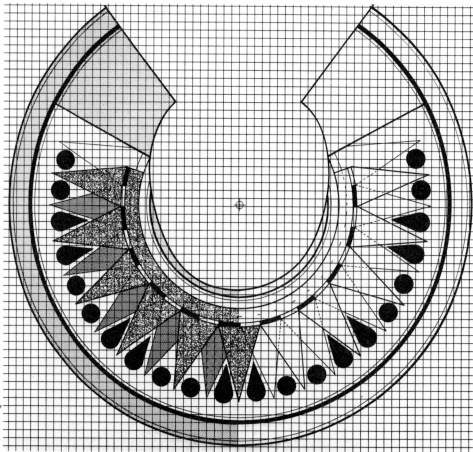

Cartoon 1 square = ¼″

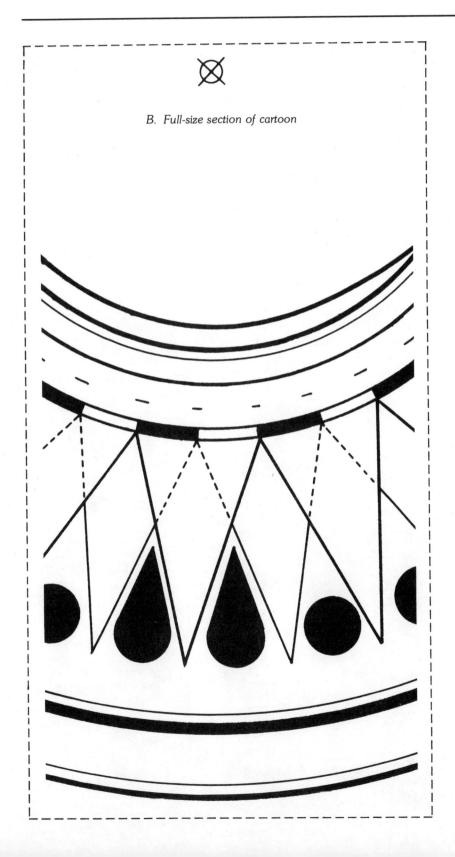

B. Full-size section of cartoon

5. Now you will paint the cream-colored imitation suede. On the graph paper you used to cut out the collar, carefully cut out the rust-colored points. Cut along the dotted lines between points—this area will be covered later by the turquoise fabric. Your upper line of cutting is the upper dotted line.

6. Spray adhesive on the back of the cut tracing paper. Let it dry until sticky, then smooth into place on the cream-colored imitation suede. Cut out the contours of this piece, which does not cover the entire soft collar (see cartoon). If you are not familiar with textile paints, practice on your doodle cloth. Paint the rust sections with textile paint. When the paint is dry, carefully remove the paper. You will re-use the paper, so set it sticky side up where a child or cat won't walk on it. Also remove the paper from the excess imitation suede so you can use it for other projects.

7. Carefully cut out the teardrop and circle shapes from the sticky paper. You can work from the backside. Reposition the tracing paper on the cream fabric—no additional spray is needed. Paint the teardrops and circles in blue textile paint, being careful not to slop over into the rust area. When paint is dry, remove the paper.

Project photo

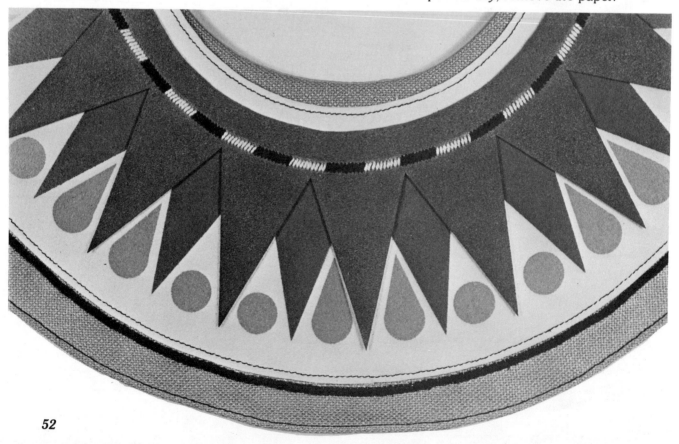

8. Position the turquoise imitation suede on the cream-colored painted fabric by spraying its wrong side with spray adhesive and letting dry till tacky before placing it on. Use your machine to mark the stitching line, as you did in the last project. Set up your un-threaded machine for a wide zigzag close together—practice on your doodle cloth to find a setting that does not rip the imitation suede. With an unthreaded machine and a wing or leather needle, stitch along the line marked on the cartoon through both layers of fabric.

9. Thread one tapestry needle with black pearl cotton and one with white. Satin stitch by hand the line you just marked, alternating colors every ten stitches and carrying the unused color behind to be covered by satin stitches as you work.

10. Lay the imitation suede in place on the linen collar. Change the sewing machine needle to a regular one (or use the special ballpoint needle made especially for imitation suede—ask your fabric store dealer about it) and load black sewing thread in the top and bobbin. With a straight stitch sew the imitation suede in place ⅛" from both edges.

11. Lay typing-weight scrap paper behind the linen. Satin stitch by machine in black at the bottom edge of the imitation suede on the linen only. The scrap paper keeps the linen from puckering and can be gently torn off when you're done.

12. Cut the black ribbon in half and lay each half ¾" from the top back edges toward the center front. Pin in place in several places so the loose ends won't accidentally catch in a seam.

13. Lay the interfacing and lining over the collar. Sew all the way around, leaving open between the marks shown on the cartoon.

14. Clip curves and trim corners. Turn collar right side out and press. Topstitch the bottom edge ⅛" from the edge.

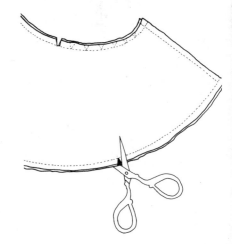

Cutting and clipping curves

ADDITIONAL IDEAS

1. For elegant gifts, use leftover scraps of imitation suede and textile paints to make nametags.
2. Imitation suede is washable. Monogram it in a washable embroidery thread and make unique place mats.
3. Blow up the pattern really huge and paint the side of your house with it.

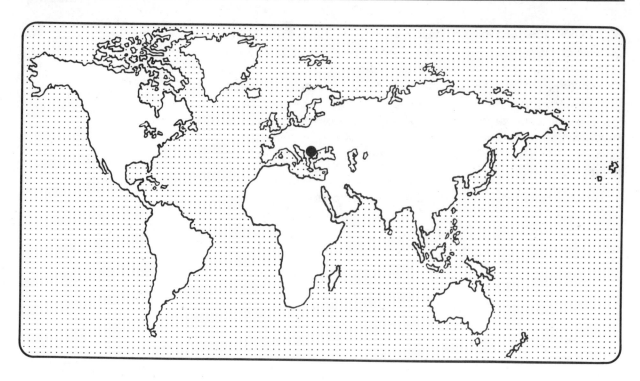

⚘GREECE

Located in the middle of the great sea routes of the Middle Ages, the Greek islands have been subject to all the struggles of civilization: traders versus pirates, Christianity versus Islam, West versus East. As a result the motifs used in embroidery rarely have any relation to island creatures—how many double-headed eagles have you heard of flapping around Greece? This often-used double-headed eagle was the imperial symbol of the Byzantine empire, which was a fertile source of inspiration for Greek embroidery. Other influences came from Italy and the Orient.

Greek folk embroidery was produced for the home, not the marketplace, and it showed the same amusing economy of work that many of us use today. If many layers of clothing were to be worn, only the parts that showed, such as hems and cuffs, were worked. If a bed cover would be half-covered by its position against the wall, it would only be half-worked. (You remember ironing only the collar and cuffs of blouses to be worn under sweaters, don't you?)

The needleworker didn't always plan well, and the motifs often didn't quite fit the space. Bands of embroidery didn't match up at the seams, and zigzags drooped. (I mention this for those of us who have never liked fractions and whose zigzags consequently always droop.)

Nevertheless, embroidery was always highly valued and passed from generation to generation. When its backing garment wore out, the embroidery was cut off and used on something else. Sometimes a garment ended up displaying bands of embroidery from several generations, a patchwork of different motifs.

In Section C, Egypt, we mentioned four categories of ornament. A study of Greek embroidery will expand your understanding of the first category, simple geometric ornament. Perhaps you will apply these ideas to your own work.

WORKING PROCESS:
Rhodes Embroidery on Tea Cosy *See also color plate 6*

Greek needleworkers were wonderfully self-sufficient in creating materials. They grew their own cotton and flax, cultivated dye plants, and raised silkworms. Their linen was medium-to-heavy-weight, perfect for pulled thread work such as Rhodes embroidery. Our design for a tea cosy is adapted from a horse on a Grecian urn 2600 years old and honors the importance that Greek needleworkers gave to negative space—that is, areas of no work next to areas heavily worked. In Rhodes embroidery, you outline the main shapes with stem stitch but work only the background surrounding that shape.

Double-headed eagle, common in Greek needlework

Project Pointers

When working the Rhodes stitch, let the thread hang down to untwist from time to time.
Use an embroidery needle for stem stitch and a tapestry needle for Rhodes stitch.

YOU WILL NEED

two 18″ × 15″ pieces (or ½ yard) of white linen (I used Moygashel)
½ yard pre-quilted lining
1 yard piping, white

1 yard white satin acetate ribbon, 1½″ wide (I used same as for section 0, Guatemala)
1 skein #5 pearl cotton, white
1 ball #8 pearl cotton, white
tapestry and embroidery needles, scissors
frame, stretcher bars, and/or hoop
doodle cloth

1. Enlarge the pattern so the bottom line of stem stitch is 11¼″ long. Transfer the pattern (including the tea cosy shape) to the linen. Mount the linen on a frame.

2. Practice the stem stitch on your doodle cloth (also mounted in a hoop), using #5 pearl cotton and an embroidery needle.

3. Stem stitch the horse and his mane. Also stitch the entire outline of the arch. Then work the horse's delicate features and bridle in #8 pearl cotton, stem stitch.

4. Begin and end with waste knots. After you are through stitching the horse, cut off the knots and wind each thread end through the

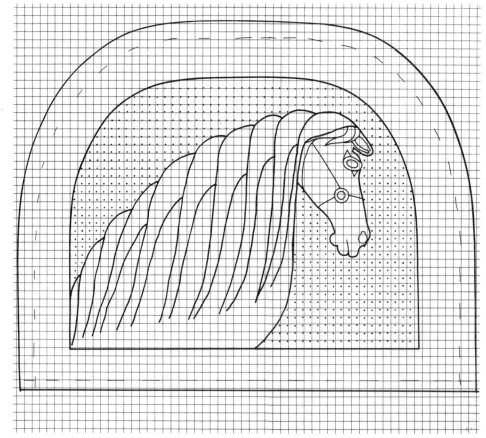

Cartoon
1 square = ¼″

56

stitches on the back. Take the time to admire the back of your work; doesn't the horse look elegant in back stitch?

5. Use #8 pearl cotton and a tapestry needle to work the Rhodes stitch in the dotted area behind the horse. Be sure to practice on your doodle cloth first. Pull each stitch tight, but don't distort the fabric. I started in the lower right corner, covering six threads of the background in each direction. (I'm glad authors need not list how many knots they must unsnarl as they work—be especially careful with newly cut threads.) Let the thread hang down from time to time to untwist.

A  B  C   D

Rhodes stitch: A. Using a tapestry needle and #5 pearl cotton, make one stitch over six threads. Pull the thread tight.
B. Make another stitch into the same holes, then move six threads to the left and repeat A-B.
C. When you reach the end of the line, drop twelve threads down (six under your last stitch and six more) and stitch right to left, two stitches to each set of holes, pulling tight each time.
D. After you've finished all the vertical work, repeat the Rhodes work horizontally between holes.

6. Finish off all waste knots on the back and take the horse off the frame.

7. Cut the two tea cosy shapes from the linen and two more from the pre-quilted lining. Sew the rounded edge of the lining, right sides together, using a ½" seam. Do not turn.

8. Using a cording or zipper foot on your machine, sew the piping to the right front side of the tea cosy (the horse side) so the stitching on the piping falls on the ½" seam line. Fold a 3" piece of ribbon in half the long way and stitch the edges together. Now put the two ends together to make a loop. Put the ribbon ends at the top center with the loop pointing down.

9. Lay the back half of the tea cosy on a flat surface, right side up. Lay the front half on top of it, right sides together. Pin and stitch on the exact line of stitching already there. Turn right side out and press.

10. Put the lining inside the tea cosy, wrong sides together. Reach inside to the top and sew a few tacking stitches to hold the two together. Fold the ribbon in half lengthwise and press. Starting in

A. Stem stitch on the underside is . . .

B. Backstitch

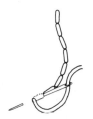

the middle back, fold it over the bottom edge. Stitch it in place by hand or machine. To end, overlap the ribbon 1″. Fold inward ½″ of the ribbon on the top and stitch in place.

ADDITIONAL IDEAS

1. Work the horse on the back of a young horse lover's jacket. If you're making the jacket, do the work before cutting out the pattern pieces. If the jacket is purchased, mount the worked panel on it.
2. Monogram an evening bag by outlining your initials and working Rhodes stitch around them.
3. Work the herb sampler in Section G, Spain, in Rhodes work, any color, outlining the bay leaf in stem stitch and working the background pattern in Rhodes stitch.

Project photo

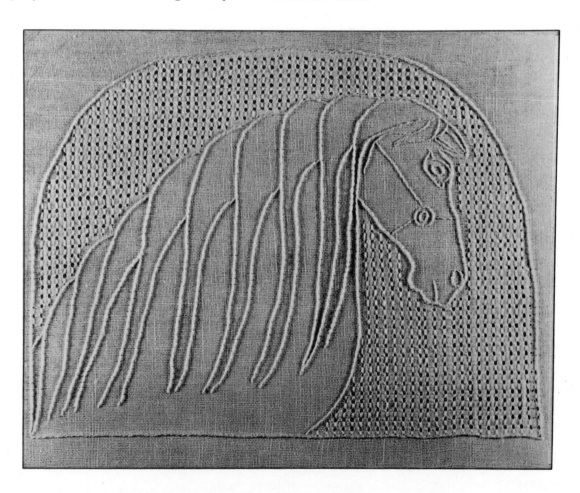

A. "Map of Middle Earth" by Patricia Ackor. Shown are three of many stitcheries celebrating scenes from J. R. Tolkien's trilogy, The Lord of the Rings—this scene is 45" × 36".

B. "Sunset from Henneth Annün," 19" × 17".

C. "Helm's Deep," 23" × 19". All photos by Rita Dyan. All photos copyright Patricia Ackor, used with permission.

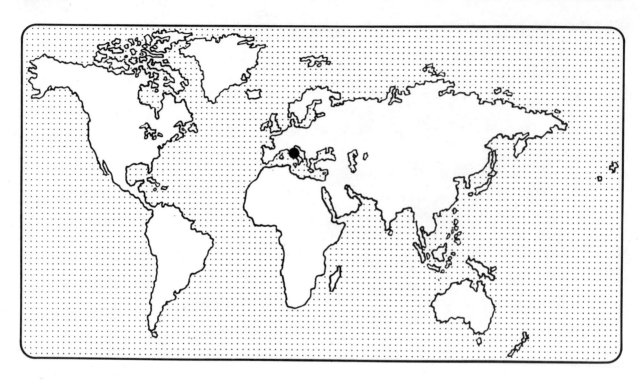

 ITALY

To prove that all embroidery is not thousands of years old and that room still exists for innovation, we've spotlighted the technique of Parma embroidery.

In the early 1900's two Italian professors developed a highly textured effect by building buttonhole stitches on top of three rows of chain stitch. The designs were often adapted from carvings in the cathedral in Parma, a small town in the province of Lombardy. These scrolls and spirals are quite striking worked in the raised line of Parma embroidery, with other stitches (chain, French knot, stem) added as accents. Traditionally the embroidery was worked on strong, heavy linen with cotton thread and used on cushions, curtains, bedspreads, and other household furnishings.

How To Make A Pomander Ball

Now that natural fibers are returning to our closets, it's fun to bring back the old tricks to make clothing sweet-smelling.

You will need
- 1 apple or small, thin-skinned orange
- 3 large boxes of unbroken cloves
- ribbon for bow
- cellophane wrap

1. Wash fruit and wipe dry. Starting at the stem end, push rows of cloves close together all over the fruit.
2. For orange pomanders, add **2** teaspoons powdered orris root (from spice department of grocery store) and powdered cinnamon. Roll the cloved orange in this mixture.
3. Let the fruit stand until the juice is dried. Wrap in cellophane and let season for two weeks. Tie a bow to the stem or a string knotted at the bottom and poked through the fruit. Hang in closet.

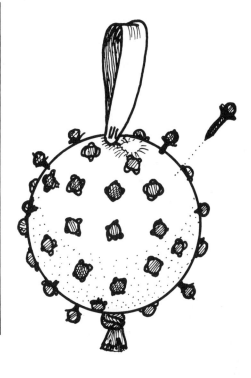

A pomander ball, made only of an orange, cloves, and a ribbon, for your closet

WORKING PROCESS:
Parma Stitch on Long Cape *See also color plate 3*

Being able to adapt designs from the world around you is a necessary skill for every needleworker. As a design source we've chosen a trim with an interwoven line that looks even more attractive worked twice as large in Parma embroidery. If you look closely, you'll realize that it is merely two doughnuts overlapped and you can create it yourself by using the circle method explained in Romania, section B, (Working Process: Wool Embroidery on Leather).

Project Pointers

Measure the front length of your cape pattern and ask the salesperson to help you buy enough black fabric for the two long strips of embroidery.

YOU WILL NEED

pattern for a full-length cape

½ yard medium-weight fabric, black

yardage as called for in your pattern (I used green linen-look fabric and pink lining fabric)

4 skeins each, #5 pearl cotton: blue and turquoise-blue

tapestry and embroidery needle, scissors

a piece of thin, stiff clear plastic or acetate (bottom of a smooth meat tray or ask at art store)

talcum powder, cornstarch, or pounce powder

rolled-up pad of felt

white pencil

doodle cloth

Cartoon   1 square = ¼"

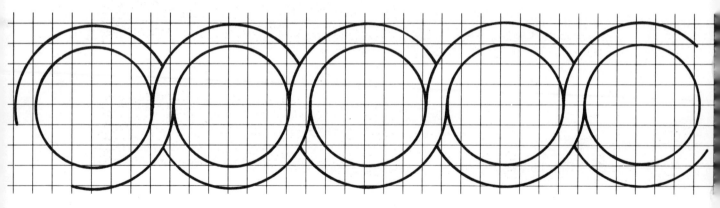

1. Cut two 5"-wide strips of the black fabric long enough to reach from the neck edge of the cape to the bottom edge.

2. Transfer the enlarged design to the plastic. An easy way is to photocopy the design and tape it to the plastic. Use an unthreaded sewing machine and a long basting stitch (6 stitches/inch) to mark the plastic. Lightly iron a long center line in the black fabric. Tape your marked plastic to the black fabric, lining up the center lines. Use the end of the rolled-up pad of felt to push talcum or pounce powder through the holes of the plastic. Carefully untape the plastic and move it down the center line. When you are done, blow off any excess powder. Then take the white pencil and play connect-a-dot. Watch the cartoon to see which line is on top when the lines intersect.

3. Fill in the lines of Parma stitch as shown to the right.

4. Put the black strip face down on a towel and press from the back.

5. Cut out the cape and lining. Lay each black strip right side up on the front edges of the cape. Baste in place. Turn the other long black edge under ⅝″ and topstitch. Finish constructing the cape and lining.

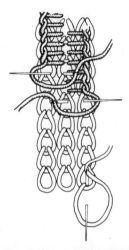

Stitch three lines of chain stitch, lining up the chains exactly. This means on outside curves the chains must be slightly longer and on inside curves, slightly shorter. With a tapestry needle, work two lines of buttonhole into the chains only, not the fabric, as shown. Put two buttonhole stitches into each chain stitch.

Project photo (designed by the authors, worked by Alberta Humphreys)

ADDITIONAL IDEAS

1. Edge a pants suit jacket with a narrow straight line of Parma stitch.
2. Work this design in greens down the center of a holiday table runner. Put different-colored teardrop candles in the centers of every other circle.
3. Work an interlaced knot in Parma stitch. (See More Bibliography: Ornament and Symbols at the end of this book for resource books where you can find knots to copy.)

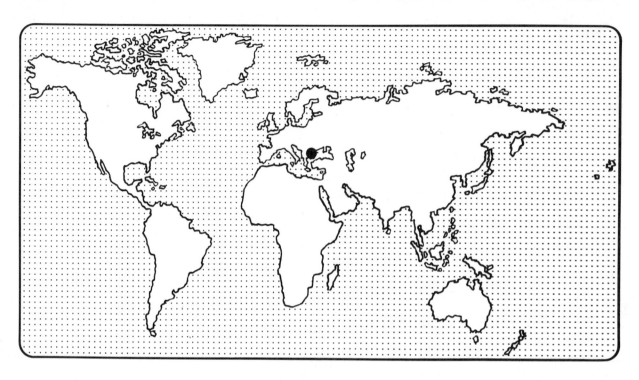

BULGARIA

Bordering on the Black Sea and Turkey, Bulgaria has always been a focal point for international East-West trade routes. Consequently needleworkers had ample supplies of linen, wool, cotton, and silk and developed over twenty variations of folk embroidery, which is a lot for a small country.

Most embroidery was worked on white garments such as shirts and flared coats called *klasniks*. The Bulgarians loved the same simple lines of embroidery found all over the world—straight, curved, broken, wavy, and spiral—yet by their characteristic color combinations, the work is distinctly Bulgarian. Often the bands of embroidery are broken by small motifs, outlines of objects from everyday life. If the motifs seem slightly Eastern in feeling, it is because five centuries of Muslim rule have left their mark.

With an average temperature of 53°F, Bulgaria is rich in plant and animal life, which also shows up in embroidery. The work has a feeling of exuberance and after studying it, I wasn't surprised to find that Bulgarians have a long-standing reputation as singers and musicians.

"The web of our life is a mingled yarn, good and bad together."

—Shakespeare

Have you ever considered the effect of needlework and textiles on our language?

some phrases:	"embroider the facts"
	"spin a yarn"
	"weave a tale"
	"unravel a mystery"
some words:	*wife* = the weaving one ("wefan" in Saxon)
	heirloom = one of the most important treasures of the house, passed from mother to daughter, was the loom
some names:	Weaver, Dyer, Taylor (I even have a friend who calls herself Gabby Goodstitch)

WORKING PROCESS:
Pattern Darning on Tote Bag

Our main design was adapted from a traditional one simply because I liked the main motif—is it a lady or a flower?

Project photo

Project Pointers

½" seams everywhere.

The lines of the graph stand for threads on the waste canvas; holes on the graph stand for holes in the waste canvas.

Each line of color symbol stands for an embroidery thread crossing over a certain number of threads.

When possible, go down into an occupied hole, come up in an unoccupied hole.

Never pierce the threads of the waste canvas.

Make sure all your embroidery threads are color-fast.

YOU WILL NEED

½ yard natural-colored duck or canvas fabric

½ yard lining (I used red)

5" × 10" rectangle of waste canvas, 9 pairs/inch

1 skein each, #5 pearl cotton: red, light and dark brown, blue, turquoise (I used #8 pearl cotton, 2 threads in each needle, but #5, one thread, is better—use what you have as long as it is color-fast)

frame or stretcher bars (optional)

scissors, sewing machine, tweezers, ruler

doodle cloth with waste canvas

1. Cut the duck as shown above. Tape or machine zigzag the edges of the duck. Decide whether you will work both sides of the tote or just one. The directions here are for one side only.

2. With your ruler measure a line parallel and 2½" from the bottom edge (which is the shorter side of the rectangle). Iron this line into the fabric. Now fold the two long sides together and iron the vertical center into place.

3. With sewing machine thread, baste waste canvas onto the duck with the blue lines parallel to the vertical center line. Make sure one long white thread lies exactly on the bottom line you ironed in and one blue thread lies next to the vertical center line. We want holes of the waste canvas on the center line, not threads. With a pin, mark the vertical center holes.

Stitch diagram

4. Mount the fabric in your frame or stretcher bars. (If you have neither, you can still stitch, but watch that your tension remains even.) Be sure in lacing that you leave enough room for your hands to work right up to the edges.

5. Practice Bulgarian darning on your doodle cloth (to which you have also basted waste canvas). Lay down all the colors for at least a few stitches. Then wet the material to make sure all your colors are color-fast.

6. Cut a dark brown thread twice as long as you normally use. You will begin stitching in the center bottom line. Pull half of the brown thread from the topside to the bottomside. Now stitch out from the

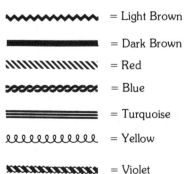

∿∿∿∿∿∿∿∿	= Light Brown
▬▬▬▬▬▬▬	= Dark Brown
＼＼＼＼＼＼＼＼	= Red
∞∞∞∞∞∞∞∞	= Blue
═══════	= Turquoise
ℓℓℓℓℓℓℓℓℓℓ	= Yellow
✗✗✗✗✗✗✗✗✗	= Violet

center to your left, following the cartoon. Thread the other half of the brown thread and stitch out to the right. Do not pierce any threads of the waste canvas or you will not be able to remove it later. This first line of dark brown stitching is very important, as all other lines of stitching are aligned from it. Notice that the second, fourth, sixth, and eighth lines of dark brown stitching are identical.

7. From now on work will be easier if you use extra needles, one threaded with each color. Begin and end with waste knots in a direction that will be covered by the darning. If possible, come up to the topside through an unoccupied hole and down into an occupied hole. This pulls the embroidery threads already there down to the underside instead of bumping them up unpleasantly.

8. All the colored threads (except the dark brown) in the upper and lower darned borders should be worked in a block of nine lines at a time, instead of all the way across the tote one line at a time as you did with the dark brown thread. Begin and end with waste knots.

9. When you have finished the two borders, work the center motifs. I worked them one motif at a time, starting with the central motif.

10. Put the spots of red, yellow, and lavender in last. I felt as though I were adding jewels. Since the bag is lined, you can carry threads across the back. (Otherwise you would have to weave them in and out on the back.)

11. When all the embroidery is done, turn the work sideways or upside-down, and examine it to be sure you haven't skipped any stitches.

12. Without taking the work off the frame, wet it with a damp sponge (or use an old clean window-cleaner bottle). Let the water soak in for a minute, then use the tweezers to remove the waste canvas. Slide the threads out; don't pull up on them or the embroidery will distort. Let the work dry on the frame before taking it off.

Constructing the Tote

13. To construct the tote, put the right long edge of the side strip on the topside of the front piece along its right (as you look at it) side. Stitch down with a ½″ seam. Leave the needle in the fabric ½″ from the bottom corner, raise the presser bar lever, and clip the fabric so you can turn the corner. Bend the side strip along the bottom edge of the tote. Clip the next corner and sew up the remaining side.

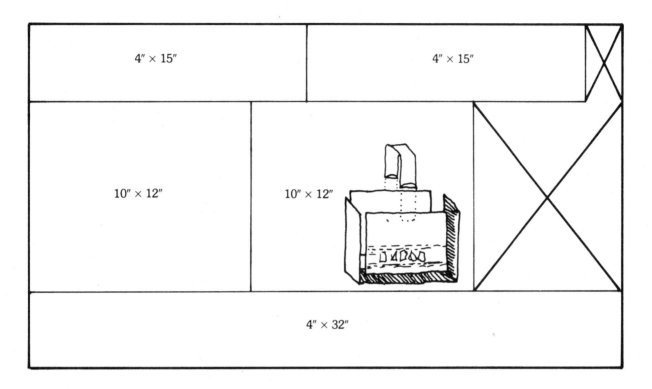

4″ × 15″	4″ × 15″

10″ × 12″	10″ × 12″

4″ × 32″

Layout of material

14. Repeat step 13 for the back half of the tote. Turn the tote inside out and press.

15. Cut out the lining except for handles. Construct it exactly like the tote, but don't turn it.

16. To make a handle, lay a 16″ piece of string or strong thread down the long middle of one handle. Lay the other handle piece on top and stitch around three sides—½″ seams on the sides and ⅛″ on the end. Clip the corners. Now pull on the string to turn the handle inside out. Cut off the string. Press.

17. Put the lining inside the tote. Iron under ½″ on the top edges of both lining and tote. Place the handles in position at the center front and back. Slip stitch the lining to the tote. Then topstitch ¼″ from the top edge.

ADDITIONAL IDEAS

1. Work one of the central motifs on an eyeglass case.
2. Use these colors in the Mexican cross-stitch design (page 131).
3. Make a bargello belt on #10 canvas with Persian wool, using the border design stacked horizontally to the desired width of your belt.

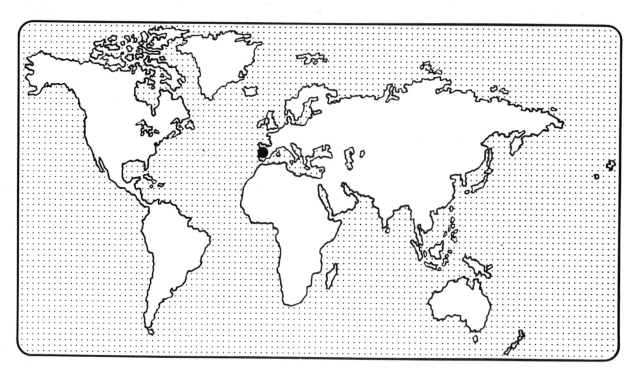

SPAIN

You would expect to find bright colors in the clothing and the needlework of sunny Spain (as in Mexico), but most of the people put the gay colors on animal trappings and choose black for themselves. Eight centuries of Moorish Mohammedan rule (and their forms of embroidery) plus this preference for black yields blackwork, a technique of embroidering black geometric patterns of varying tone on white linen.

The Mohammedan religion forbade the portrayal of living creatures in art, so putting the emphasis on "no *living* creatures," the Spanish embroidered animals with heads separated from bodies by a collar. The severed head meant the animal wasn't alive.

The Moors made arid land fertile through irrigation, and flax was cultivated abundantly for years in Spain, until the Moors left in 1492. During this time, linen embroidery flourished. To this day, well-watered land is called "tierra de linares," that is, "flax land."

In those early days linen was so common that people yearned for that expensive, exotic fabric: cotton. Every Spanish girl hoped for a few cotton sheets for her dowry (if you've ever slept on a linen sheet, you'll agree with her—scratchy!). That same wishful girl was considered educated when she'd learned her catechism for confirmation and when she knew her stitches and proved it by making a sampler. Since there were no pattern books like the one you're reading, the sampler was a record of stitches and variations.

Spanish needleworkers kept to a few stitches but combined them in an endless variety of patterns. Many of these patterns were developed from the mosaics and tiles of the Moors (which in turn had come from Rome, Greece, Persia, and Egypt). The patterns were also used in wood carvings, plaster on ceilings, and exterior architectural details, so the overall effect was of a pleasing unity.

Sometimes the adaptation of an Arab pattern was done with no understanding of its meaning. For example, in one blackwork embroidery the olive branch in a bird's bill was next embroidered in the mouth of a monster and then in the tail of a fish!

Blackwork itself cannot be said to have originated in Spain, since it has been worked in many countries for many years. Some people trace its entry into England to the arrival from Spain of Katherine of Aragon (1501), but blackwork had been there all along. True, at first the English court ladies didn't like its "melancholy aspect," but soon it became the rage. The same is happening today.

In the English court black silk was used as an embroidery thread; in Spain undyed wool from black sheep was used more often.

The most important aspect of blackwork to study is tone, or density. It isn't enough to sprinkle pretty patterns inside a shape. Study light and shadow on your face. If a picture is taken of you with the sun hitting you full-face, you look ghastly. If the light shines from the side, however, you look interesting, with highlights on your cheeks and shadows defining your nose and eyes. Likewise in blackwork, design with areas of light pattern, medium pattern, and dense pattern. If blackwork intrigues you, start a design scrapbook of black-and-white photographs—buildings, scenery, animals, gardens—to help you plan your own work.

WORKING PROCESS:
Blackwork Kitchen Picture *See also color plate 6*

Many of us spend hours a year in the kitchen. What better place to hang a sampler of the new blackwork patterns you've learned? We love to cook with fresh herbs and have designed a blackwork sampler of all our favorites, one of which is shown here—bay.

Spanish blackwork, one strand natural black wool on white linen. Collection of the University of California, Berkeley Design Department Textile Teaching Collection.

Project Pointers

Stab stitch in a frame for best results.
Tie the silk to the needle's eye for easier handling.

Project photo

YOU WILL NEED

10″ × 13″ rectangle of white aida cloth, 11 blocks/inch
3 spools size D sewing silk (also called buttonhole twist) or #8 pearl
  cotton, black
1 skein #5 pearl cotton, black
hoop or frame
masking tape, scissors
mat and frame
doodle cloth

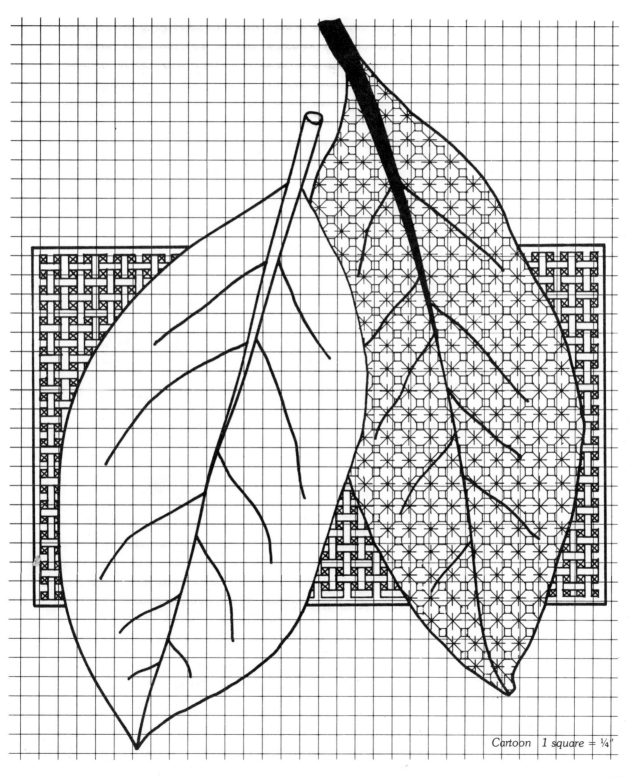

Cartoon | 1 square = ¼″

1. Tape the edges of the aida cloth with masking tape. Transfer the outlines of the bay leaves and the outline of the rectangle behind them.

2. Put your doodle cloth in a hoop and practice pattern B, using size D sewing silk and the tapestry needle.

Pattern A Put in (1) the crosses first, then (2) horizontal lines, then (3) vertical lines to make (4) the complete pattern.

3. Mount the rectangle of aida in the frame. Stitch the lattice pattern first. Silk is slippery so it helps to tie the end to the needle eye. This does not interfere with stitching.

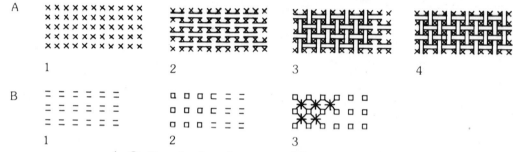

Pattern B Put in (1) horizontal lines first, (2) vertical lines next, and last (3) the star, which is two crosses on top of each other.

4. Outline the bay leaves in #5 pearl cotton and the embroidery needle. The outline and center stem of the leaf on the left are worked in stem stitch; the outline of the leaf on the right, in back stitch, as are the veins on both leaves. The heavy black stem on the right leaf is worked in (what else?) stem stitch in close rows. Also work the letters in stem stitch.

5. Now fill in pattern A with the silk and a tapestry needle.

6. Outline the rectangle in double running stitch with #5 pearl cotton and the embroidery needle. Be sure to stab stitch.

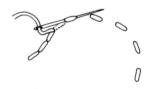

Double running stitch: Stitch a row of running stitch clockwise. When you meet yourself, turn around and stitch running stitch counter-clockwise, covering all the gaps. Use an embroidery needle and stab stitch, straight up and down for each stitch.

7. Remove from stitching frame, mat, and frame.

ADDITIONAL IDEAS

1. Copy the pattern of your kitchen flooring (or any geometric pattern you like) onto graph paper. Use this as a chart to develop a blackwork picture for your kitchen wall.

2. Put your child in front of a blank wall. Shine a light at his or her profile, adjusting the shadow to whatever size you're willing to work. Copy the shadow silhouette (on paper, not the wall). Develop the silhouette in blackwork.

3. Take a black-and-white picture of your house. Have it printed large. Transfer it to graph paper. Develop the light and dark areas in blackwork.

"Nicho" by Ann Spiess Mills, three-dimensional stitched creche scene drawn from the artist's Spanish-German background combined with the images of the Santinos (saint-makers) of the American Southwest.

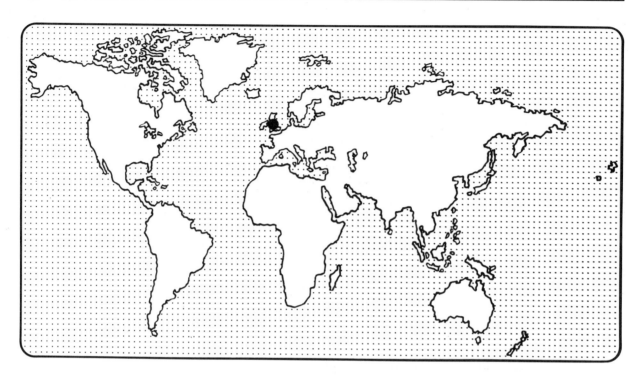

 ENGLAND

The easiest clothes to make are those that require little shaping. Take a length of fabric, gather in the fullness at the neck, add another rectangle for the sleeves, and gather in its fullness at the wrist. Sew it up, and you have an English smock, worn by working people to protect their clothing.

Embroidery on top of the gathers, along the connecting bands, and on the collars developed in the 1800's. It's interesting to see the same primitive geometric designs we mentioned in Eskimo, Egyptian, and Bulgarian art—that is, spirals, waves, circles—used in a different way in England. The embroidery designs on the side bands were often stamped on by metal blocks. You can borrow this same technique of marking fabric for embroidery by dipping small cookie cutters in cornstarch or talcum powder, if your fabric is dark or patterned, and in powdered charcoal, if the fabric is light. Choose cookie cutters with simple shapes such as hearts or circles.

For a time, each embroidery design on an English smock signified a specific trade, such as shepherd or milkman, and the smocks were worked by the family for the family, being carefully passed from generation to generation. Then about 1880, artists and travelers began to collect the smocks, so a market developed for the manufacture of them. These smocks were not cheap, costing about one week's pay, but anyone who could afford it bought two, one for work and one for special occasions.

A cottage industry developed, giving women the chance to make a few extra pennies. On Monday mornings a man would bring the most experienced embroiderer in the village a cartful of fabrics. She would pencil in the embroidery and smocking designs and hand out the material to the village women. On Fridays the cart would collect the handwork and the smocks would be finished elsewhere by machine. In one family the husband had to get up at 3 A.M. to deliver farm goods, while the wife stayed up working on smocks until time to awaken her husband. Then she would fall into bed, poor cross-eyed lady.

Traditionally the smocks were made of medium-weight linen or cotton twill in white or cream with embroidery in the same color. The trades that were more apt to get dirty while working, such as cowmen, wore blue or dark brown smocks and saved their white smocks for Sunday.

The smocks were often cleverly made the same front and back, so they could be reversed and worn longer before washing. This is similar to today's backpacker who, conscious of extra weight, takes one T-shirt. The first day (s)he wears it front forward; the second, backwards; the third, inside out. After that, fellow travelers usually demand a laundry stop.

Why did the smock disappear? The Industrial Revolution brought machinery to the fields, and the voluminous folds of the smock were liable to catch in machine parts, making the smock dangerous to wear (you remember Isadora Duncan's scarf?).

WORKING PROCESS:
Smocking on Long Hostess Apron *See also color plate 10*

Today making a linen smock would be both tedious and expensive. Although transfer dots are sold to mark fabric for gathering, we do not recommend using them on anything but tightly woven fabrics. The smocking will not hang right on linen and other fabrics.

It is far easier to use a fabric screened with a regular pattern, such as gingham. Our design uses the traditional idea of protecting work clothing by smocking a long hostess apron in a large plaid fabric. The embroidery on the shoulder straps can be worked by hand, but it is faster to work it by machine.

Project photo

Project Pointers

Depending on the weight of your fabric, plan on 4″ gathering into 1″.

Make sure the gathers are absolutely lined up before smocking.

YOU WILL NEED

1 yard 45″ wide red 1″ gingham-plaid cotton fabric
1 yard cotton lining fabric (I used pink)
⅝ yard red cotton fabric
1 skein each, #5 pearl cotton: white and red
1 ball #8 pearl cotton, white
embroidery needle, scissors
1 spool button and carpet thread or crochet cotton
lightweight interfacing
masking tape
doodle cloths for both red and plaid gingham

1. Practice gathering and smocking on your doodle cloth.

2. For the front smocked piece, cut a piece of gingham plaid 32″ × 11″ and a piece of lining to fit it. This will give you a 1″ margin on each side. Put the lining behind the gingham and treat these fabrics as one. Use the button and carpet thread to run lines of running stitch across the plaid gingham, making even stitches about ¼″ apart. Use your finger or a slip of paper to help you space these

Linen smock with feather-stitched embroidery. Photo courtesy of Royal Ontario Museum.

stitches—they must all be lined up in vertical rows or the gathers will hang unevenly. (Why doesn't somebody manufacture a needle with ¼″ marks on it so we can baste accurately?) Start your line of running stitch with a knot in the right 1″ margin; end by leaving a long unknotted tail of thread in the left 1″ margin, by which you will later gather the fold. Make 11 lines of running stitch 1″ apart, following the lines of the gingham plaid. If possible, work on a flat surface, and if you make a mistake in lining up stitches, take it out or the folds will not hang right.

3. Pull up all the gathering threads and knot them. Use the eye of the needle to coax the folds of the gathers into place; they should line up exactly. Some people say that you should plan on gathering 3″ into 1″ but on lightweight material, it's more like 4″ into 1″.

4. Work the embroidery on the top edges of the folds as shown on the cartoon in #5 pearl cotton. Each pattern is set off by two rows of stem stitch, one red and one white, with the red always on the light side of the fabric. To help you line up rows of chevron and cable stitch, you can put a line of masking tape across the fabric for a straight edge. Start and end with three or four backstitches in the margin—knots will not hold in washing. Try to use a thread long enough to last across the row but if you run out, make backstitches on the back in the folds.

5. When you are done, remove all the gathering threads except the top and bottom ones. You can leave the threads in, but it has a softer feeling if they're left out.

6. Cut four 5″ wide strips as long as your red fabric is wide (mine was 45″). Take one of these strips and cut it into two 5″ strips of equal length. These will be the shoulder straps. Iron each strip in half the long way. Place them in front of you with the folds pointing out and the raw edges toward the center. Mark the front side of each with a pin. Now open up the two strips and back the two front edges with strips of lightweight interfacing.

7. The apron straps can be done by hand or machine. I'll describe the machine method. Load the #8 pearl cotton into your sewing machine bobbin. Choose one of your machine's decorative stitches and set up the machine for it. Use regular white sewing machine thread on the top. Stitch with the pellon side up in four long rows of stitching, the outer two 1″ from the stitching line (you have ½″ seam) and 1″ from the fold; the inner two each 2″ in. When you turn the fabric over, the crochet cotton is laid on the topside. You did practice this on your doodle cloth, didn't you?

Stem stitch

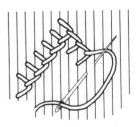

Feather stitch

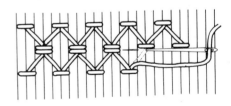

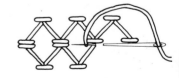

Chevron stitch

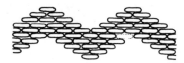

Wave stitch

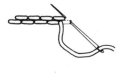

Cable stitch

8. To work the straps by hand, embroider four long rows of any stitch—stem on the outside and feather on the inside would be nice.

9. Cut a strip of red fabric 1½" wide and as long as your smocking is wide. Press under ¼" on each side. Press the strip in half. Cut off the smocking ½" from the top embroidery line. Hand stitch the red strip of fabric to the top of the smocking on both the outside and inside.

10. Turn under the ½" seams on the shoulder straps and press. Hand sew them to the sides of the smocking. Topstitch the rest of the straps by machine, turning the ends in.

11. For the lower apron, cut a large rectangle of plaid gingham and lining as wide as you wish (mine was 31" × 37"). Gather it at the top. (I'm being loose about the directions here because I'm skinny and you may not be—change the size to fit you.)

12. Fold two more of the 5" strips in half lengthwise. Press under the ½" seams. Sew by machine to the two long edges of the lower apron.

13. Cut a strip of red fabric 1½" wide and as long as the bottom edge of the lower apron plus ½" on each side. Press the strip in half lengthwise; press in the ½" on each end; press in the ¼" seam allowance on the long edge. Topstitch into place along the bottom.

14. Cut the remaining 5" strip of red fabric in half *lengthwise* so you have two 2½" strips. Back one strip with lightweight pellon. Fold the ends of this strip together to find the center front and lightly press it in. Press under ½" seam allowance on the long edges of both strips. Right sides together, hand stitch one side of the red strip to the lower smocking edge, using a ½" seam. Find the center front of the lower apron and match it to the red strip. Right sides together, stitch it by machine with a ½" seam. Press. Match the second red strip to the sewn one, wrong sides together. Topstitch everywhere but the smocking area (the foot on the machine doesn't travel smoothly over the gathers), which should be hand stitched.

ADDITIONAL IDEAS

1. Work two long narrow strips of smocking and insert into the sleeves of a blouse.
2. Use the new stitches you've learned in a geometric pattern on a linen collar like the Egyptian one.
3. Make a pillow sampler of all the smocking stitches you can dig up. It's a fun way to learn new stitches.

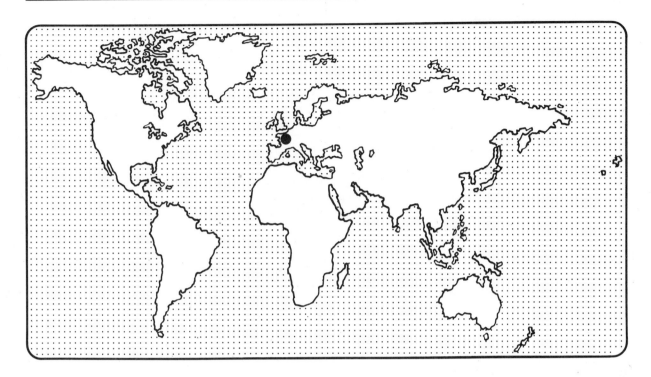

FRANCE

In the seventeenth century, to the chagrin of the French court, the center of the lace industry was Italy, specifically Venice.

Cardinal Richelieu, minister to King Louis XIII, wished to halt the flow of money out of France. At first he imposed a high tax on Venetian lace, but when it became clear that the French aristocracy would still buy lace, Richelieu attempted to replace it with a product equally desirable but all French. Richelieu imported lace workers from Venice, set up workshops, and encouraged innovation.

The result was a form of cut-work that is called the link between lace and embroidery: *point de Richelieu* or Richelieu cut-work. Worked on fine white linen with white cotton thread, islands of design are outlined with buttonhole stitch, anchored to the main fabric with thread bars, and then the channels between are cut away.

Like Cardinal Richelieu's interest in cut-work, France's involvement in embroidery has often been linked to her political history. As mentioned in the beginning of this linen section, one of the most

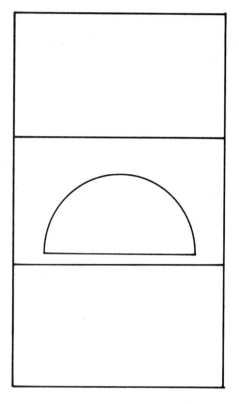

Purse layout

important embroideries in the world is France's Bayeux Tapestry, 231' long and 19½" high. It was embroidered to commemorate the Battle of Hastings in 1066, when William the Conqueror defeated Harold of England. Figures of soldiers and horses are embroidered in wool on linen, using stem stitch and couching. Richelieu cut-work became a folk art when the French Revolution abolished the distinction between royalty and commoners.

WORKING PROCESS:
Richelieu Cut-work Purse

Combining Richelieu cut-work with the typically French way of layering borders, we've designed a peacock framed in lace for an evening purse. The peacock sits in front of a pocket in which fabric is inserted to match the color of your dress. When you change dresses, you can put a different color behind the pocket. In this way you will be able to use the purse for years, in keeping with the ancient belief that the flesh of the peacock never decayed—making it a symbol of immortality.

Project Pointers

Work the first part of Richelieu cut-work in the hoop and the buttonholing without a hoop.

Cartoon   1 square = ¼"

YOU WILL NEED

¼ yard white linen as finely woven as you can find (mine is 42
   threads/inch, a garage sale table runner in good condition that I
   promptly cut up)
13″ × 8″ rectangle of lining
assorted white lace trims at least 8″ long
1 ball, #8 pearl cotton, white
hoop, scissors sharp to the point, embroidery needle, thimble
doodle cloth

1. Cut two rectangles of linen, one 13″ × 8″, the other 8″ square.
Transfer the peacock to the 8″ square 2⅛″ above the bottom edge.
Mount the fabric in your hoop.

2. Practice Richelieu cut-work on your doodle cloth. Then make the
peacock pocket. Outline all the peacock feathers in running stitch,
buttonholing all the bars as shown above.

3. Work the peacock body in satin stitch (padded, if you like). Put
three little French knots at the top of his crown. The center lines of
his proud feathers are worked in back stitch and the circles at the
top in buttonhole.

4. Remove the hoop. Buttonhole all around the peacock feathers,
with the continuous part of the buttonhole stitch toward the area to
be cut out (see cartoon). Take tiny neat stitches side-by-side.

5. From the front, cut through the linen behind the buttonholed
bars. Then turn the linen over. Roll the cut parts back toward the
lines of buttonhole. Carefully cut off excess linen. Don't do this part
if you are tired, grouchy, or if the light is poor.

6. Press the peacock face down into a towel. Spray starch on the
back makes a nice finish. Trim 1½″ off the top and bottom of the
peacock pattern, making it 5″ × 8″. Turn under ¼″ on the top and
bottom edge—press. Turn under another ¼″ on both edges, and
topstitch ⅛″ from the top edge.

7. Measure 4½″ from either end of the large linen rectangle and
fold toward the center. Press. Open the rectangle flat. Lay the
peacock on the center third. Topstitch ⅛″ from its bottom edge
through the peacock pocket and the rectangle.

8. Lay the assorted white lace trims across the rectangle, stitching
each in place.

A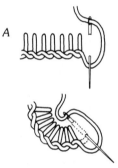

B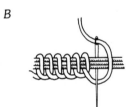

*A. Buttonhole stitch (straight and
in a curve)*
B. Making Richelieu bars

Satin stitch

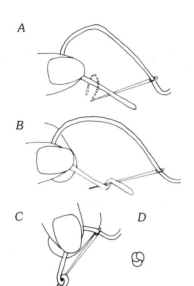

A

B

C   D

French knots

Project photo

9. Lay the lining rectangle on top of the linen rectangle, right sides facing. Stitch around the edges with a ½″ seam, leaving an opening for turning. Clip the corners and turn. Press.

10. Turn the third of the purse under the peacock toward the lining. Hand stitch the two sides together to make an envelope purse.

11. For the fabric insertion behind the peacock, press a rectangle of iron-on interfacing to the back of a 6″ × 3½″ piece of your dress fabric. Insert in the peacock pocket.

ADDITIONAL IDEAS

1. Work the design for Parma embroidery (section E, Italy) in Richelieu cut-work on a table runner.
2. Substitute fine linen for the Egyptian collar and work Richelieu cut-work at the teardrops and circles.
3. Enlarge the peacock to the size of your TV screen. Embroider the outlines of the peacock in stem stitch and do Rhodes stitch around it for a TV cosy.

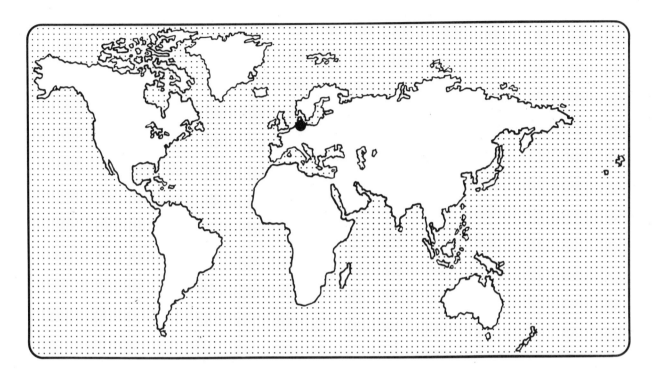

DENMARK

One major aspect of life we North American needleworkers take for granted is the amount of light in which to work. In Denmark, closer to the North Pole, the nights are longer and the days shorter during the cold, indoor months of the year. With lighting always a problem, then, an interesting variation of embroidery developed. Threads were withdrawn from parts of homemade linen fabric, and the remaining threads were rearranged in pleasing patterns. This work could be done by moonlight, saving the more complicated surface stitching for the day.

Called Hedebo, this technique originated in the stretch of heath ("hede") west of Copenhagen, where lived ("bo") farmers who grew flax for linen. By the time a person plants, cultivates, harvests, spins, and weaves flax into linen, (s)he is bound to take pride in whatever final use is made of that linen. Hence, almost all household items and clothing were richly decorated with embroidery by the Danish women.

In fact the whole process of flax into linen played an important

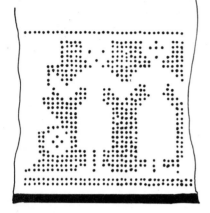

A typically Danish motif is the "little people" used in borders. These two were taken from an eighteenth-century cushion and were originally worked with punch stitch only, and were less than one inch high, on fine linen.

social role. Before a young suitor proposed marriage, he carved for his love a special wooden tool used in the preparation of flax. She, in turn, made her betrothed a special linen wedding shirt with elaborate embroidery on the collar, front, and cuffs. If she were to embroider a shirt for another man, it would be considered an infidelity.

These embroidered articles were true folk needlework, in that they were made solely for the home and had no market value outside Denmark. The women found time in a busy day to embroider, just as we do. Often a woman would stay up all night to finish a piece.

> "When I'm a grown-up woman,
> With hair up on my head,
> I'll sit and sew till very late,
> And never go to bed!"
> —from (*Tools and Toys of Stitchery*, Gertrude Whiting, 1928)

There is something addictive about working Hedebo. The drawn-thread portion seems to be particularly so, and you may find yourself working the same stitch pattern over with "just a little change of tension" many more times than you planned. This can exasperate family members who haven't been hooked by Hedebo.

Flora Klickmann in her charming book, *Cult of the Needle,* relates the story of a Danish girl who was helping her family clear stones in a field. Her job was to dig a pit for the stones. She quickly dug the pit and then pulled out some Hedebo embroidery hidden in her pocket because her father did not like this "fancy-work." She became so engrossed in her needlework that she didn't see him approaching until too late. Hoping he hadn't seen her, she threw the fabric in the pit and covered it with dirt, meaning to recover it later. He had seen and was outraged. Without a word, he rolled stones into the pit and covered the embroidery forever with earth.

It has often been pointed out that the richer the soil anywhere in the world, the finer the embroidery standards there. How did fine Hedebo develop among the peasants? In Denmark it may have happened this way. Before the Protestant Reformation embroidery was taught in the religious houses of the Church. When the Reformation disbanded these houses, embroidery moved to the manor houses. Where the soil was rich, the farmers were prosperous. The farmers' wives could afford servants, which gave the women time to produce fine needlework for the home. To supply her demand for embroidered articles for the home, a lady would teach her daughters and maidservants how to stitch. Then the maid would carry this knowledge back to her home and friends and as a result, fine needlework like Hedebo was found in peasant homes.

WORKING PROCESS:
Hedebo Valentine Pincushion *See also color plate 8*

Many years ago pins were hand-made and thus quite precious to the owner. To guard against loss, pins were stored in boxes. In the sixteenth century, as pins became more easily produced, pincushions replaced pin boxes.

Today we can simplify Hedebo embroidery by using linen canvas rather than linen fabric. This eliminates the need to remove threads from the backing in order to pull the threads together. Make this small pincushion to give to someone you love (perhaps yourself?) on Valentine's Day.

Project Pointers

Holes on the graph paper stand for holes on the canvas;
    lines on the graph paper stand for threads on the canvas;
    drawn lines on the cartoon stand for embroidery threads.
Work pulled-thread projects on a frame.

YOU WILL NEED

7″ square scraps of organza and flannel
9″ square frame plus 6″ or larger embroidery hoop
9″ square piece of linen needlepoint canvas (or any canvas), 13 holes/inch
6″ × 12″ lining fabric in contrasting color (I used red)
1 ball heavy white crochet cotton (4-ply)
1 skein #5 pearl cotton, white
masking tape, ruler, staple gun or thumbtacks
tapestry and embroidery needles, scissors
sand to fill pincushion
doodle cloth of linen needlepoint canvas

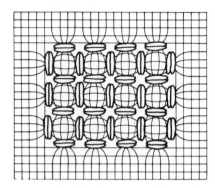

Punch stitch—this is worked the same as Rhodes stitch (Fig. D-3)

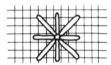

Star stitch—eight stitches from the outside to the center hole, pulling tight

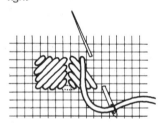

Diagonal satin stitch

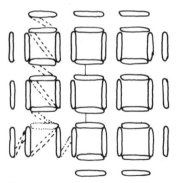

Cobbler stitch—work the vertical stitches first over four threads, spacing them: stitch/skip two vertical threads/stitch/skip four/stitch/skip two/stitch/skip four. Then work the horizontal stitches in the same way, pulling all threads tight.

1. Tape the ends of your canvas so the thread won't catch on it. Staple or thumbtack the canvas to the frame.

2. Find the center hole of your canvas by measuring it with a ruler. Mark with a pin. Mark top of frame with a pin so you don't get confused. Practice each stitch section on doodle cloth—it's no fun to rip out mistakes. All the pulled thread stitches are worked with crochet cotton and a tapestry needle.

3. Work the punch stitch in the center of the heart, starting at the lower left or right side. This is the same as the Rhodes stitch in section D, Greece. Follow the graph on the cartoon.

4. Count 33 threads out from the center hole in four directions to find the perimeter of your work. Mark with pins. Find the four corners and mark with pins. Stitch the satin stitch all around, mitering the corners as shown in the cartoon.

5. Stitch the four corner units, following the cartoon.

6. Stitch the area under the heart. Notice that you are using the diagonal satin stitch again, but getting a different effect by pulling it tight.

7. Now you'll stitch the satin stitch around the heart separately. Transfer the design to organza or, if you'd like a plumper stitch as I did, put organza behind white flannel and transfer the design by the photocopy method mentioned in the introduction. Put organza and/or flannel in an embroidery hoop. Cut the outlines of the heart and teardrop shapes out of the photocopy and tape to the flannel. Using #5 pearl cotton and an embroidery needle, satin stitch the teardrop shapes right over and through the paper. (I wish satin stitch over paper were my original idea but it's been used for centuries.)

8. With the work still in the hoop, cut out the center of the heart, through the paper, flannel, and organza. Then cut around the outside of the satin stitches, leaving ⅛″ margin. Pin the heart in place on the Hedebo frame (see cartoon). Use #5 pearl cotton and a tapestry needle to satin stitch the inner edge of the heart to the linen canvas. I backed the canvas with organza and viciously split threads of the canvas to get a good edge.

9. Backstitch around the teardrop shapes to secure them to the canvas. If you want, trim the flannel closer to the edges of the teardrops, although it isn't necessary.

10. Finish the pincushion by cutting two lining pieces in a contrasting color, each 6″ square. Take the canvas off the frame. Put one

Cartoon

Stitch key (* = pull tight)

1 Star
2 Diagonal Satin
3 Cobbler
4 Punch

piece of lining behind it, so the color will shine through. Put one piece of lining on top of it, right sides together. Sew ½″ seams around the edges, leaving an opening for turning. Trim corners and excess canvas. Turn right side out and press. Fill with sand and slipstitch closed. (Better yet, have a talented artist and collaborator build you a box for it, so it looks spectacular.)

Project photo

ADDITIONAL IDEAS

1. Inset this design into the bodice of a special dress.
2. Work pulled thread on those handy tote bags with needlepoint canvas flaps that are sold in needlework stores.
3. Use this same design on even-weave linen for a scrapbook cover. You can work the satin stitch teardrops right on the fabric instead of separately.

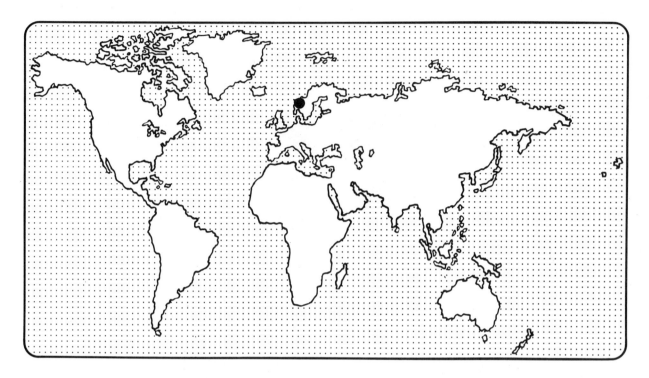

NORWAY

The form of embroidery is often dictated by both its use and its backing fabric. In Norway these two elements combined to give us the beautiful white embroidery called Hardanger. This technique is worked on double-thread open-weave linen fabric (i.e., Hardanger cloth) using blocks of satin stitch, called "klosters," to define areas that will later be cut away. The linen material demands angular designs like triangles and squares. Used on the national costume, these angular forms fit best in wide borders on aprons, kerchiefs, and blouses, but when Hardanger was used on other articles, its form was continued, even though it didn't necessarily have to be a border.

Originally, Hardanger was worked on hand-spun, hand-woven linen. The peasant communities around the fjord of Hardanger in western Norway were entirely self-supporting. Even though there is little land good for cultivation, they grew their own flax, sheared sheep, and collected dye plants. The living room was also a work room, with a spinning wheel and a loom taking up much of the space.

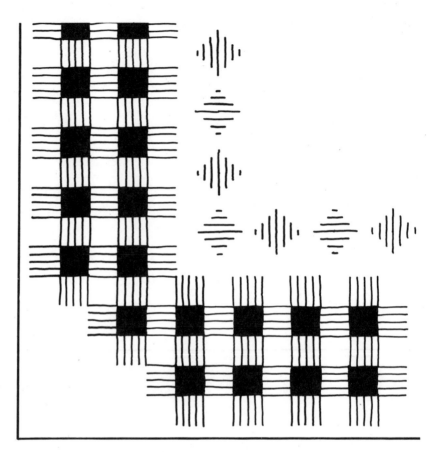

Hardanger techniques are ideal for border treatments on placemats, tablecloths, and curtains. In this design, cross-shaped klosters with cutaways are combined with darning.

Despite this self-sufficient isolation, some of the motifs of needlework show a startling Assyrian and Egyptian influence. This can undoubtedly be traced to the famous Vikings and their forays into Europe and down as far as Constantinople in Turkey. The much-used eight-pointed star, for example, that many people equate with Scandinavian design, is also frequently found in India. Even today, the Norwegians are a seagoing people and they have more sailors and ships at sea in proportion to their population than any other nation.

WORKING PROCESS:
Hardanger Greeting Card *See also color plate 10*

In some districts of Norway there is a long-standing tradition of giving embroidered presents—a bride gives one to her mother-in-law, a godmother to her godchild. This idea, combined with the traveling spirit of the Norwegian sailors inspired us to design an embroidered holiday card to send to far-away loved ones.

Project Pointers

It's easier to count threads when the light comes from the
side rather than straight onto your fabric.
No knots—start with a waste knot; end by weaving ends in.
Use a hoop.
Cut only areas bounded by four worked sides facing the
center.
Each hole on the graph stands for a hole on the Hardanger
cloth; each line on the graph stands for a thread on the
cloth; each drawn line stands for an embroidery stitch.

YOU WILL NEED

6½″ × 13″ piece of white Hardanger cloth, 18 blocks/inch
1 skein, #5 pearl cotton, white
tapestry needle
hoop
masking tape
shirt cardboard, matboard, small amount green and silver paper,
    rubber cement, X-acto knife or razor blade, ruler
sewing machine thread, scissors
doodle cloth (part of 13″ above)

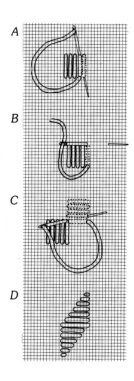

A-C. How to make kloster blocks
D. One arm of the star

1. Practice Hardanger on your doodle cloth mounted in the hoop.
Do not split the threads of the Hardanger cloth. Begin with a waste
knot; end by weaving threads under on the back.

2. To help you count, outline the outside shape (4″ × 5″) in sewing
machine thread, running stitch. This will later be removed.

3. Count 20 threads from the top and 20 threads from the left side
to find the center *thread* (not hole) of the star. Mount the fabric in a
hoop. Embroider star and its rays first, working from the center out.
As you finish each part of the star, slide the needle under the stitches
on the back to return to the center. Let the thread hang down and
untwist periodically. Turn the hoop as needed, so that you are
laying stitches either horizontally or vertically, whichever way you
like better.

4. Work the klosters blocks at the bottom, turning the hoop as you
work. Slide the needle under worked areas on the back to get from

Cartoon

one place to another. Make sure no thread goes across any part that will be cut out.

5. Study the cartoon; only areas that are secured by four sides

facing a center can be cut. Cut out the squares carefully with good scissors. Double check each cut before you cut.

6. Cut a 5″ × 5¾″ rectangle out of the shirt cardboard. Trim the Hardanger to the same size. Lay it face up on the shirt cardboard and lightly trace through the holes in the klosters blocks. Remove the Hardanger. Cut a small square of silver paper slightly larger than one of the pencilled squares. Rubber cement it to the left square on the second row, so it will fall under the star's rays. Cut a piece of green paper big enough to show through the remaining holes without obscuring the silver paper. Rubber cement in place.

7. Rubber cement the back of the Hardanger and stick it to the shirt cardboard. Make sure the colors show through the right places. Smooth it down.

8. Cut an 11″ × 6¼″ rectangle from the matboard. Measure the halfway point of the long edges. Place ruler across it and draw the X-acto blade lightly along the ruler, scoring the line without cutting through. Move the ruler just off the center line and make a second score. Now the card will fold in half.

Project photo

9. On the front half of the card cut a 4″ × 5″ opening. Rubber cement the outside ½″ of worked side of the Hardanger. Press it in place behind the mat frame you just made. If the basting stitches show, remove them. Let dry overnight, weighted by this book. Write a message inside the card and send to people you like.

ADDITIONAL IDEAS

1. Work this design in colors against a white background.
2. Substitute needlepoint canvas for Hardanger. Work the cut-out centers in basket-weave or half-cross stitch and the star and klosters in upright Gobelin (or satin stitch).
3. Go back to a lost era: make a full-sized tablecloth in Hardanger. The two types of klosters used in this project can be put together to form striking borders.

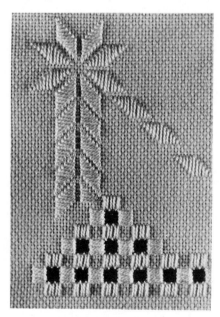

SUPPLIES AND BIBLIOGRAPHY—LINEN

Dewey Decimal library call numbers given in parentheses when known

Linen

Leggett, William F. *The Story of Linen.* New York: Chem Publishing, 1945.

Belgian Linen Association, 280 Madison Ave., New York, NY 10016.

Frederick J. Fawcett, Inc., 129 South St., Boston, MA 02111—linen yarns, free price list.

Glenshee Fabrics, Richmond Brothers, Balfield Road Works, Dundee DD36AJ, England—send self-addressed envelope and $1 for brochure on their beautiful even-weave linen.

Egypt

Drury, Allen. *Return to Thebes.* New York: Doubleday, 1977—fiction.

Houston, Mary G. *Ancient Egyptian, Mesopotamian, and Persian Costume and Decoration.* London: Adam and Charles Black, 1920.

Westendorf, Wolfhart. *Painting, Sculpture, and Architecture of Ancient Egypt.* New York: Harry N. Abrams, 1968 (709.3).

Greece

Gentles, Margaret. *Turkish and Greek Island Embroideries.* Art Institute of Chicago, 1964.

Hadjimichalis, Angelica. *Patterns of Greek Decorative Art.* National Organization of Hellenic Handicrafts, 1969.

Bulgaria

Lang, David Marshall. *The Bulgarians.* London: Thames and Hudson, 1976.

Tschukanova, Rossiza. *Bulgarische Volksstickerei,* Verlag Balgarski Hudoshnik, 1957.

Spain

Geddes, Elizabeth, and McNeill, Moyra. *Blackwork Embroidery.* London: Mills and Boon, 1965.

Gostelow, Mary. *Blackwork.* New York: Van Nostrand Reinhold, 1967. $12.95 (746.44).

Scoular, Marion. "Blackwork." *Leisure Arts,* 1976. $2.

Stapley, Mildred. *Popular Weaving and Embroidery in Spain.* Madrid: Editorial Voluntad, 1924.

England

Buck, Anne. "The Countryman's Smock." *Folklife, Journal of the Society for Folklore Studies,* vol. 1, 1963.

Cave, Oenone. *English Folk Embroideries.* London: Mills and Boon, 1965.

Hart, Natalie. *English Peasant Smock.* 1973. $4.25—she publishes an

1 / Persian Resht embroidery

backpack (page 150)

2 / Closeup of Persian Resht embroidery (page 150)

4 / Egyptian patchwork on wallet (page 35)

5 / Canadian button blanket (page 169)

6 / Upper left: Portuguese shadow appliqué curtains (page 183)

lower left: Greek Rhodes embroidery on tea cosy (page 55)

right: Spanish blackwork picture (page 71)

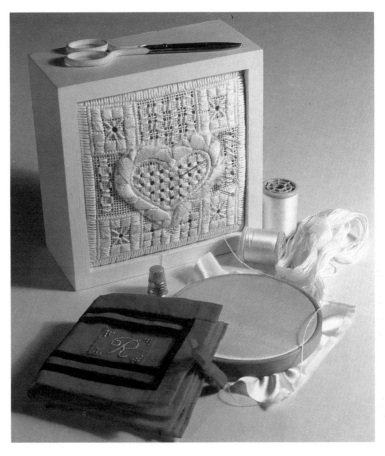

8 / Danish Hedebo Valentine pincushion (page 87)
Thai Meo appliqué needlecase (page 187)

7 / Panamanian mola panel on denim jacket (page 120)

9 / Maltese tufted Christmas centerpiece (page 160)

11 / *Swedish free embroidery on pillow (page 157)*

excellent catalog of other ethnic patterns. Write Clifton Park Plaza, Mechanicville, NY 12118.

Embroiderers' Guild of England, 18 Bolton St., London WIY 7PA, England—*Embroidery,* their quarterly magazine ($8/year) is excellent.

Little Miss Muffet, 6709 Glenbrook Dr., Knoxville, TN 37919—patterns for smocking kits. Write for free list.

Denmark

McNeill, Moyra. *Pulled Thread Embroidery.* New York: Taplinger, 1971. $4.50 (746.4).

Meyer, Ann. "Pulled Thread on Canvas." *Leisure Arts,* 1976. $2.

Danish Handicraft Guild, 38, Vimmelskaftet, Copenhagen K, Denmark—they put out a charming quarterly magazine in English and Danish.

Norway

Quinn, Elvia. *Beginner's Hardanger,* $2; *Hardanger Embroidery* and *Round and Ecclesiastical Hardanger,* each $5.50 (self-published), 108 5th Ave. NW, Wells, MN 56097—she also sells finished pieces and charts.

Stewart, Janice S. *The Folk Arts of Norway.* Madison, WI.: University of Wisconsin, 1953.

"Synthesis II" by Bea Miller, 8' × 5', solid wool stitchery that took two and a half years to complete and is a visual statement about the seed of life.

part three ✖ COTTON

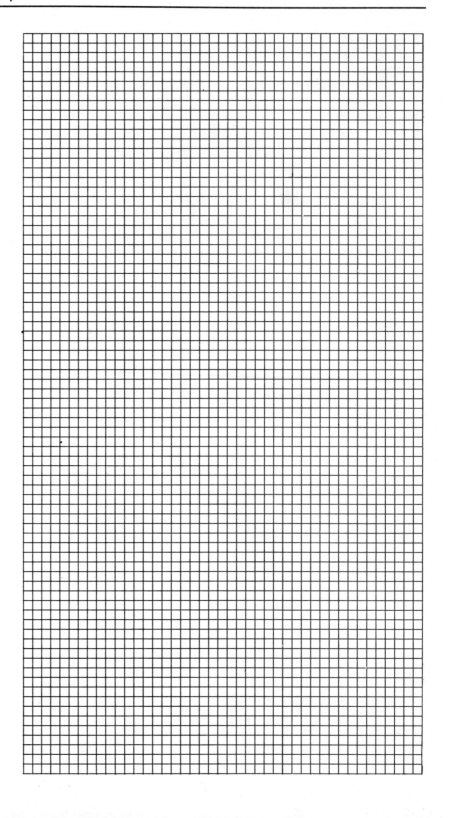

Cotton has always been so universally linked to India that when Columbus stumbled ashore in the Bahamas in 1492, he declared he'd reached India. Was that not cotton growing? Well, then, it *must* be India.

Columbus wasn't the first person to make mistakes over cotton. Way back in 330 B.C. Alexander the Great's wanderlust took him through Central Asia and down to India, where cotton had already been cultivated for more than 400 years. Alexander returned to Greece with samples of this exciting new fiber, but he neglected to do much research into its cultivation. As a result, his official historian, Herodotus, reported that in India, there were "trees which grow wild, the fruit whereof is a wool exceeding in beauty and goodness that of sheep. The natives make their clothes of this tree-wool."

15th century drawing of sheep

If it's in print, it must be true, right? Operating on this principle, 1700 years later, a German artist drew the mysterious Scythian sheep that grow on a shrub in soft downy pods. Each pod had a flexible stem so the sheep could lean down and eat grass, but the sheep died when all the grass was eaten. The wool of these sheep was, of course, cotton.

Actually, that fifteenth-century German artist must have had a sense of humor as cotton, both fabrics and cultivation, reached Europe by 200 A.D. At the time of the Crusades (1096–1270), a lively trade in cotton yardage made many a Christian soldier richer. But it was the Portuguese explorer, Vasco da Gama in 1497 who paved the way for cotton in the Western world. In opening a water route to India, he made possible a wide-scale cotton trade.

Following the course of cotton before and after that is merely tracing human history: How did the cotton industry get to England? The same revocation of the Edict of Nantes (1685) that helped linen across the channel moved the cotton industry there, through the manufacturing efforts of the Flemish refugees. Soon the cotton empire was irrevocably yanked away from India by two eighteenth-century British inventions, the spinning jenny and the power loom.

By a quirk of history, one year the cotton empire was based in England; the next, 1793, it shifted to the United States, and all because Eli Whitney had invented the cotton gin, which made easy the cleaning of dirt and seeds out of the cotton balls.

No longer did one person plant, cultivate, harvest, clean, spin, dye, weave, and embroider cotton. Specialization and textile mills came with the Industrial Revolution. In fact, the early growth of New England was the story of cotton mills being built, people moving closer to the new factory, and the need for more mills. At that time, if anyone had predicted the rise (and fall) of cotton in the U.S. South, (s)he would have been ridiculed.

But of course the cotton empire did shift to the South and where it will go in the future is unknown. Cotton is called a universal fiber because it can grow almost anywhere in the world. It always has been, and undoubtedly always will be, closely tied to the ups and downs of human history. Do not be surprised if some cotton seeds are taken along by today's explorers, the astronauts, to the first space colonies.

SOME FORMS OF COTTON*

Fabrics
finely woven: lawn, batiste, dimity, dotted Swiss, organdy, voile
medium-weight: broadcloth, chambray, chintz, flannel, gingham, sateen, seersucker
heavy-weight: corduroy, denim, duck, poplin, terry, velveteen, batting
Threads
extra-fine: 100% cotton machine embroidery thread
medium-weight: 100% cotton sewing machine thread, six-strand cotton embroidery floss, pearl cotton (the larger the number, the finer the thread), retors à broder, crochet cotton
heavy-weight: roving

*Note: New forms of fabric and thread are constantly being developed. Keep in touch with your local fabric and needlework stores.

CARE OF COTTON

Pure cotton fabrics must be preshrunk before constructing projects. This will also quickly tell you whether imported cottons are colorfast. Iron from the back with a dry iron on a dampened cloth over the cotton fabric.

Cotton-synthetic blends must be washed and ironed at a temperature no higher than the synthetic can stand. Test a scrap with the iron to find out the correct temperature.

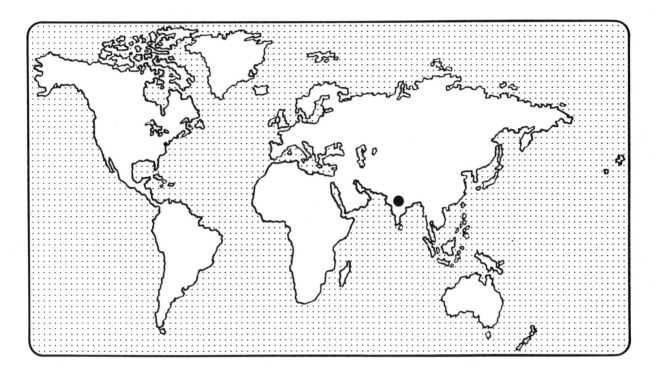

INDIA

Needlework in India is an ancient art more than 4000 years old, with fascinating historical and regional subtleties that could be studied for years. Each aspect of the art has been refined and developed over this span of years. As in dance, where every gesture stands for a concept or myth, color has come to have an immense social and spiritual significance—for example, lime green means early summer, while saffron means spring. Another example of this extreme sensitivity of the embroiderers to their color palette is the breakdown of white into five tones: Ivory white, jasmine white, conch white, white-of-an-August-moon, and white-of-August-clouds-when-rain-is-spent.

Mirror embroidery is found in many parts of India, but it is usually associated with Kutch in the western state of Gujarat, which is a lonely desert area populated by small communities of farmers and cowherders. Originally the embroidery held precious gems and metals, but today small flakes of mica are used, evidence of less prosperous times. Still the brilliant colors and flashing light prompt

Indian purse with shisha, cross stitch, and interlaced herringbone, from the collection of the Lowie Museum of Anthropology, University of California, Berkeley. Worked in a square and then three corners folded and sewn together to make an envelope.

descriptions like that of Theophile Gautier in the nineteenth century: "Indian embroidery seeks to engage in a contest with the sun, to have a duel to the death with the blinding light and glowing sky . . . . At all costs its duty is to shine and glitter and to send forth the prismatic rays; it must be blazing, blinding and phosphorescent—and so the sun acknowledges defeat."

The Indian legend of how weaving and embroidery began makes a charming bedside story for children and grandchildren. (For a livelier story, substitute your child's name for the young weaver's.) Once upon a time people did not wear clothes because they did not know how to weave. Hambrumai was a young child with sharp eyes. She sat quietly by the river and watched the waves ripple lightly on its surface. When she looked up at the trees, she noticed the patterns of the interlaced branches. The gentle god Matai rewarded the observant child by teaching her how to weave. Hambrumai used the patterns she had seen in nature in the beautiful clothes she wove and embroidered for all her friends. Happily, her designs turned into butterflies and today we can see Hambrumai's patterns as the markings on butterfly wings.

> **Cotton *is* India; Indian towns where cotton is made often were adapted into English as words for particular kinds of cloth.**
>
> | | |
> |---|---|
> | bandanna | gingham |
> | calico | khaki |
> | chintz | pajama |
> | dimity | sash |
> | dungaree | shawl |

WORKING PROCESS:
Shisha Embroidery on Food Cover

Combining the idea of Hambrumai's butterfly patterns and mirror embroidery, we offer a small tent to cover your picnic food while you're watching ripples on the river. You can use the mirror technique in your own work to secure any small object to a backing— polished stones, driftwood, fake jewels.

> *Project Pointers*
>
> **Shisha mirrors are washable.**

YOU WILL NEED

7″ × 33″ strip of white cotton fabric (an old sheet is fine if not
  threadbare)
⅜ yard red cotton fabric
1¼ yards orange piping
1¼ yards pink ribbon (½″)
⅜ yard lightweight interfacing
1¼ yard boning or wire for bottom edge
1 skein each, 6-strand embroidery floss: orange, pink, and yellow
16 round shisha mirrors
6″ embroidery hoop
sewing needle and white sewing machine thread
tapestry and embroidery needles
doodle cloth

Project photo (designed by the authors, worked by Pat Bliss)

1 square = ¼″   Cartoon

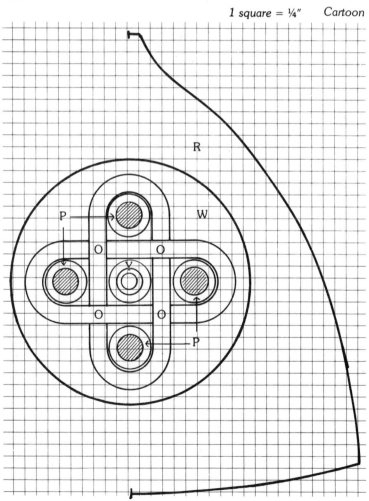

Color Code

Threads

Color and Stitch

O = Orange: Herringbone

P = Pink; Shisha

Y = Yellow; Buttonhole

Fabrics

R = Red

W = White

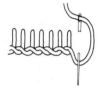 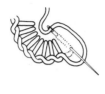

Buttonhole stitch

Herringbone stitch

1. Transfer the butterfly design and the outer circle of the medallion five times to the white fabric, leaving 1″ between each medallion. (Iron-on transfer pencils make this easy, and the extra medallion is for practicing on.)

2. Mount the white fabric in your hoop, centering a medallion. Don't forget to practice on your doodle cloth (which is the extra medallion).

3. Using two strands of the pink floss, secure the four mirrors to the white fabric as shown above. Start and end with three small backstitches toward the center behind the mirror.

4. Stitch the rows of double herringbone in two strands of orange floss.

5. Stitch two circles of yellow buttonhole from the center out.

6. Press the embroidery floss face down into a towel. Cut out the four medallions adding a ½″ seam allowance all around. Cut out four medallions of the lightweight interfacing without a seam allowance. On the embroidered medallions baste ¼″ from the outside edge. Put the interfacing behind the embroidery, and pull up the basting stitches so the white cotton snuggles over the edge of the

A. Put two vertical stitches over the mirror, close to its middle. Add two horizontal stitches, wrapping them around the vertical stitches. This is the cage to hold the mirror.
B. Come up at the edge of the mirror at A and do a buttonhole over the cage.
C. Go into the fabric at B and make a chain stitch, keeping the thread under the needle.
D. Take another buttonhole over the cage and . . .
E. Another chain.
F. Repeat buttonhole/chain sequence around mirror.

A   B 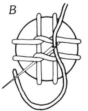 C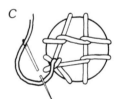

D 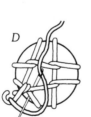 E 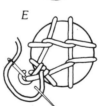 F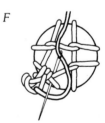

interfacing. Cut off any excess folds outside the basting stitches so the medallion will lie absolutely flat.

7. Cut out the four red panels of the food tent. Cut them out of interfacing, too, and back each red panel. Sew the four medallions in place 2″ above the bottom edge.

8. Sew the orange piping to the left edge of each red panel, using a ¼″ seam. Right sides together, sew all four panels to each other.

9. Cut a 3″ length of ribbon and fold it in half to make a loop. Reach in and push ½″ of the ribbon ends through the top hole of the food tent. Sew across the top of the tent, ¼″ from the edge. Turn the food tent right side out and press.

10. Fold the ribbon in half lengthwise. Fold it over the bottom edge and stitch it in place by hand or machine, leaving 2″ open on the back to insert the boning or wire. Close gap by hand. Put the food tent over a plate of fresh brownies, and save one for me!

ADDITIONAL IDEAS

1. Pretty the pocket of a purchased pinafore with the shisha shine. (I've been listening to Gilbert and Sullivan as I stitch.)
2. Work a giant floor pillow with a meadow of flowers and butterflies, all with shisha centers.
3. Use the Romanian design and colors (see section B, p. 38) for a yoke but work shisha in the middle (surrounded by buttonhole).

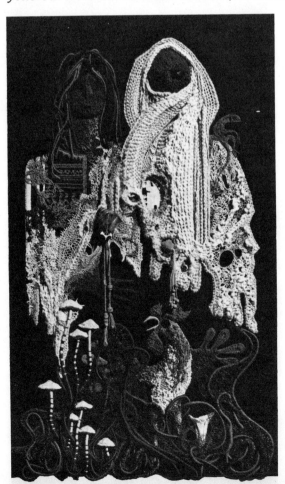

"Las Curanderas" by Wilcke Smith—refers to a highly respected and powerful person in the Mexican Indian community who breaks spells and evil eye and is especially good with love spells—24″ × 48″, three hidden leather fetish pouches, removable wand, needleweaving, surface stitchery, wrapping, and crochet. Photo courtesy of the artist.

113

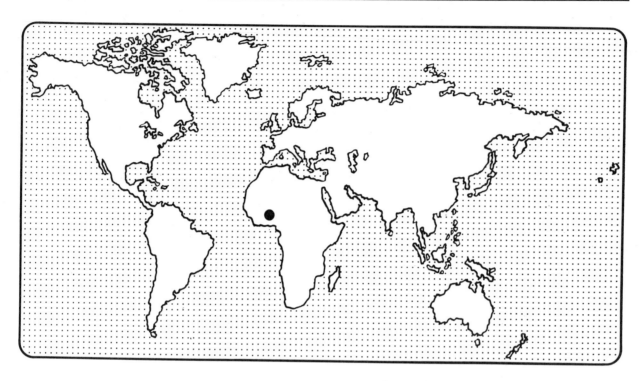

WEST AFRICA (GAMBIA)

The sewing machine brought a quiet revolution to clothing in West Africa. Before, only the very rich could afford the heavily embroidered floor-length over-robe called a "warramba." Worn by both men and women, the garment was a symbol of social status. Requiring more than ten yards of cotton damask, it was hand-couched in intricate designs that identified the family and were carefully handed down, along with the robe, from generation to generation.

But the arrival of the sewing machine made the embroidery available and affordable to all. Today tailors in West Africa (particularly Nigeria and Gambia) sit out in the street with their treadle machines, visiting with neighbors as they cut, assemble, and decorate the garment you've ordered. And you can ask for anything that pleases you—if a passing warramba catches your fancy, the tailor can match it, borrow a motif from it, or interpret it for you. The machine-embroidered designs are seemingly made freehand, as no line is marked to follow on the fabric, but careful examination reveals that the patterns are simple circles and spirals piled on top of each other.

WORKING PROCESS:
Machine Embroidery on Tunic

West Africans are progressive and inventive. Liberian women, for example, began extracting blue ink from Peace Corps ditto sheets to dye the traditional rice bags. It is not surprising then, to find the sewing machine used so cleverly in Gambia. Our design is based on circles the size of a quarter. Like the West Africans, we too will use the sewing machine cleverly, by placing a bold thick thread in the bobbin and stitching from the back side of our material. This way we can use threads far thicker than can fit through the needle.

Imported shirt from West Africa, worked in free machine embroidery on sewing machine from underside so that bobbin chain stitch is laid on topside. Collection of Kali Koala Fanning.

Project Pointers

Put the hoop on backwards for free machine embroidery. Remember to lower the presser bar lever before you stitch (easy to forget in free machine embroidery).

YOU WILL NEED

½ yard black medium-weight cotton fabric
pattern for man's tunic or caftan
yardage for tunic as called for on pattern
1 ball fine crochet cotton or buttonhole twist, white
sewing machine (zigzag not necessary)
sewing machine thread; black and white
snaps, tapestry needle, scissors
tracing paper, felt-tipped pen
6–8″ embroidery hoop
doodle cloth

1. Cut a 12″ × 13″ piece of the black cotton. Later you will trim it to size.

2. Transfer the cartoon to the tracing paper. Pin the cartoon to the underside of the black fabric (the 12″ goes from side to side).

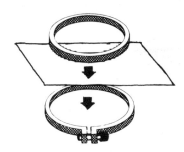

Put the hoop on backwards— outer ring first, then fabric, then inner ring.

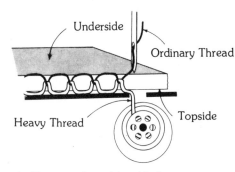

A. To use a thread too big to go through the needle, load the thread in the bobbin and stitch underside up.

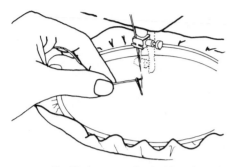

B. To bring up the bobbin thread, hold the top thread securely in your left hand and turn the hand-wheel toward you one revolution. Yank gently on the top thread to bring the bobbin loop up; pull it all the way through. With the presser bar lever down, stitch several times in one place to lock the threads. Cut off ends.

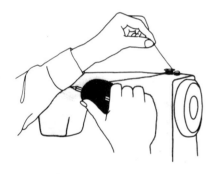

To wind thick threads onto the bobbin, put a pencil through the center of the spool and use your fingers to guide the thread evenly.

Use your middle fingers to press the fabric against the needle plate and your thumbs and pinkies to guide the hoop. The fabric must always be flat against the needle plate.

3. Load crochet cotton onto your bobbin by hand (or through the largest-eyed needle you have, if you have a self-winding bobbin). Put white sewing thread on the top.

4. Set up your machine for free machine embroidery: Take off the presser foot, put on the darning foot if you have one (it's optional), lower the feed dogs (optional), and set the stitch length to 0 (the point between forward and reverse near "Fine"). Tighten the top tension slightly.

5. Put the hoop on the doodle cloth—backwards, as shown above. Practice free machine embroidering on your doodle cloth. Check the side with the crochet cotton to be sure the top tension is correct. The crochet cotton should lie on the surface smoothly. If loops of the sewing machine thread show, tighten the top tension more.

6. Put the hoop on the black fabric with the tracing paper up. At the shoulder seam line pull up the bobbin thread as shown above and lock the threads. Slowly and smoothly stitch along the cartoon. When you run into the hoop, raise the presser bar lever, and pull the hoop away from the needle. Cut the threads at least 3″ long. Pull the crochet cotton to the cartoon side, either by gently tugging on the sewing machine thread and pulling the bobbin loop through or by threading the tapestry needle with the crochet cotton and stitching it through to the cartoon side. Go back to the shoulder line and stitch as much of the second line of spirals as is within the hoop. End as you did for the first line.

7. Carefully remove the hoop without tearing the cartoon and move it along the stitching lines. With a 6″ hoop you can do all the stitching in three hoop moves plus one for the medallion. As you stitch in a new area, hold the thread ends from the previous area across a spiral so they will be secured by the new line of stitching.

8. When done, trim the fabric to the neck and shoulder lines. Carefully tear off the cartoon paper. Tweezers help get the smaller pieces. Anything you can't extract will disappear after the first washing, so don't worry. Press ¼″ under on three sides (not the neck).

9. Cut out the rest of the tunic in whatever yardage you chose. Lay the black worked piece, crochet cotton side up, on top of the front. Topstitch around the three pressed-under sides, ¼″ from the edge.

10. Construct the garment as directed in your pattern instructions. However, if you choose to have the tunic close at the shoulder as we did, only sew 1½″ from the shoulder in of the left shoulder seam. Turn the remainder in, press, and topstitch. Then sew snaps to the shoulder seams for closing.

ADDITIONAL IDEAS

1. Work the medallion in the center of a pillow, surrounded by a border of several rows of the spirals (which are derived from the shape of a quarter).
2. Use the spiral pattern on a bookmark.
3. Combine the medallion with shisha mirrors (as worked in Section L, India) for a purse.

Cartoon   1 square = ¼″

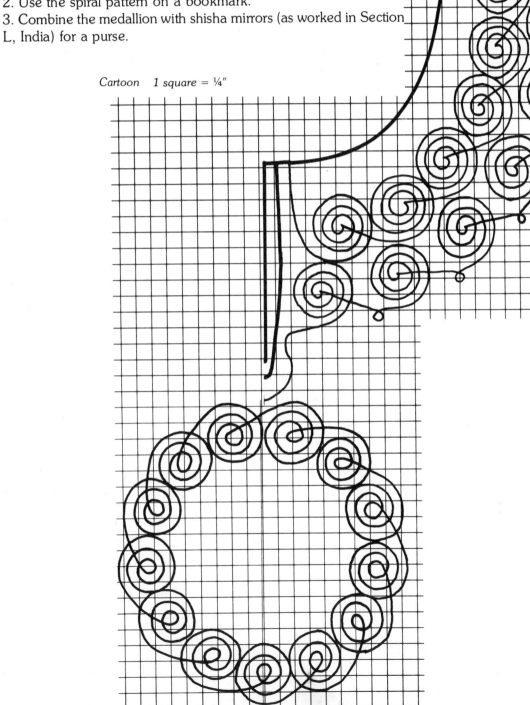

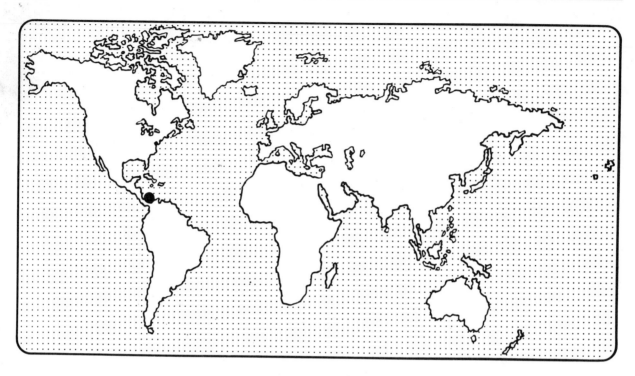

 PANAMA

As we've mentioned over and over in this book, the story of textiles is the story of people—birth, death, love/hate, war/peace, and weather are the abiding elements. We often live as if we've reached the end of the story, as if all changes have been made and life will always be the way it is right now, today. But the "what if's" continue to affect us and our needlework. What if the big earthquake California is waiting for strikes the East Coast instead? What if Lake Michigan freezes solid and all Great Lakes transport stops?

The molas of the Cuna people off the east coast of Panama reflect the what-if's of their lives. The designs began as body painting in the late 1600's, changed to cloth painting under the disapproving noses of the French Huguenots, and when machine-manufactured cloth became available in the mid-1800's, developed into the unique form of layered appliqué so famous today. At first the designs were geometric or stylized animals, but around 1940 advertising motifs from cigarettes and magazines began to show up in the work. When a tidal wave wiped out their coast homes, the Indians moved to the San Blas Islands, a canoe-ride off the Panama coast. They still have to paddle to the mainland for fresh water. Even today, the Indians live a simple community life on islands no bigger than football fields, which makes the dazzling complexity of the molas even more surprising.

At first the molas were connected by painted-cloth yokes into blouses. Each woman took great pride in the intricacy of her needlework. If she made it too easy, with wide lines between motifs, the others teased her, calling it a grandmother mola—meaning her eyesight was poor. When outsiders became interested in collecting molas, the designs became less detailed.

The Indians have been avid traders for 400 years. If you have the chance to buy a mola, the unseen mark of a good one is that the top layer should be continuous, allowing the panel to stretch in all directions. And remember, these were originally made to be worn, not hung on walls, as is increasingly the custom here.

A Cuna woman wears a mola while she makes another. Photo by Carol S. Dilfer.

WORKING PROCESS:
Mola Panel on Denim Jacket *See also color plate 7*

Our design is appropriate for a teenager's denim jacket, so you might want to share this folklore with your offspring. Cuna marriage is arranged by the father. The ceremony consists of kidnapping the adolescent boy and throwing him into the girl's hammock three nights in a row. After the marriage ceremony there is a period of courtship when the two get to know each other. The divorce rate is no higher among the Cuna than among Californians, though it is reported that divorces are more amicable.

Project Pointers

100% cotton fabrics turn under better than blends.
Use a flat or round toothpick to help nudge under edges.
Stitch each color of fabric in a matching color thread.

YOU WILL NEED

denim jacket
10″ × 14″ pieces of preshrunk cotton fabric (preferably 100% cotton), red, yellow, black, and a backing (I used muslin)
scraps of cotton fabric: light blue, dark blue, purple, pink, green, orange, white
sewing machine threads in all the same colors as fabrics
small amount light blue embroidery floss
tracing paper, white pencil
sharp scissors, needle
wooden toothpick (flat or round)

All unmarked = Yellow

▨ = Red

O = Orange

Y = Yellow

G = Green

LB = Light Blue

DB = Dark Blue

V = Violet

W = White

1. Cut the four main pieces of 10″ × 14″ fabric. The edges of 100% cotton fabric turn under easier than cotton-polyester blends, but use what you have.

2. Enlarge the cartoon. Transfer the enlarged cartoon to the red fabric. The easiest way is to photocopy it, tape the photocopy to a window, and tape the red fabric over it. Trace only the outline of the buffalo and all other shapes with the white pencil.

3. Stack the fabrics in this way: backing on the bottom, black next, yellow next, red on top. Baste around the outsides first, then about

Cartoon   1 square = ¼"

¼" outside the buffalo shape and between the surrounding shapes. This is to keep the fabrics from shifting.

4. Cut out the buffalo shape carefully on the inner white line. Cut *only* the red fabric. (Save this cut-out buffalo for another mola.) Trace with the white pencil onto the exposed yellow fabric the outline of the buffalo you have just cut out. Hold the edges of the red fabric with your fingers as you trace.

5. Clip curves on the red fabric but don't cut deeper than ⅛". Turn under the edge of the red fabric to the white line. Pin only a few inches at a time. Sew by hand with red thread, using a tiny overcast stitch and sewing through all layers to the muslin. Remember, this will be washed many times, so take small stitches, for strength. Use the toothpick to help you coax under the edge.

6. Cut ⅛" away from the white line you traced on the yellow fabric, *toward* the center of the buffalo. You will cut out another buffalo, shrunken, for that other mola. Clip the curves and turn under the edge. Stitch as in step 5.

7. The outer shapes are all worked in a similar manner, so I will explain only one, the upper left shape. The shape is outlined by two white lines ⅛" apart. From the red fabric only, cut out along the inner white line. Set the red shape on a dark blue fabric scrap and use it as a pattern to cut out an identical shape from the dark blue fabric. Pin together and set aside until later.

8. On the exposed yellow fabric trace the shape of the red fabric with white pencil, as you did for the buffalo. Clip the corners of the red fabric and turn under to the outer white line. Stitch.

9. Cut ⅛" away (toward the center) from the white line you made in step 8. Save the cut-out shape for another mola. Clip the yellow corners and turn under to the white line. Stitch.

10. Take the red-blue shape and make long cuts through both layers where the indentations will be (see cartoon). Make one cut between each. Trim the red fabric only ⅛" from the inner white line. Pin the two layers in place on the mola. Turn under the edges of the red fabric and stitch. Then turn under the edges of the blue fabric and stitch—you will have no guideline for the blue since its white line got turned under with the red, but it's easy to eyeball it. Make the blue an ⅛" shadow all around the red.

11. Work all the shapes this way. However, the two small pink shapes on either side will have to be copied off the cartoon before stitching.

12. Trace the shape of the buffalo and its inner lines on tracing paper. Carefully cut out the stripes, horn, and eye from the paper. Lay this stencil on the mola, lining up the buffalo shapes. With a white pencil, trace these shapes onto the black fabric.

13. Use the stencil on the various colored fabric scraps to trace the appropriate shape for that color (follow the coding on the cartoon). Cut ⅛" around each colored shape. Make one long cut per shape through the black fabric only—be careful not to cut the muslin. Slip the colored fabric behind the black fabric, turn the edges of the black fabric in and stitch with black thread.

14. Use two strands of the light blue embroidery floss to chain stitch the eyes.

15. Press under the fabrics at the outer white line of the entire mola. Hold up the red fabric so it won't be cut and trim away the other three layers on the pressed line. Turn the red fabric over the edge of the three layers. Position the mola on the back of your denim jacket and stitch it in place.

Take tiny stitches at the edge of the fabric.

I was not able to use all 100% cotton fabrics and consequently some threads refused to tuck under. However I worked this mola at a ranch in northern California and none of the 60 kibbitzers noticed the threads. They all were dazzled by the cheerful colors.

ADDITIONAL IDEAS

1. Make a pocket-sized mola with your initials.
2. Appliqué the cut-out red buffalo to a telephone book cover and stitch the rainbow lines in herringbone.
3. Use the outer shapes as appliqué blocks for a king-sized quilt.

Project photo

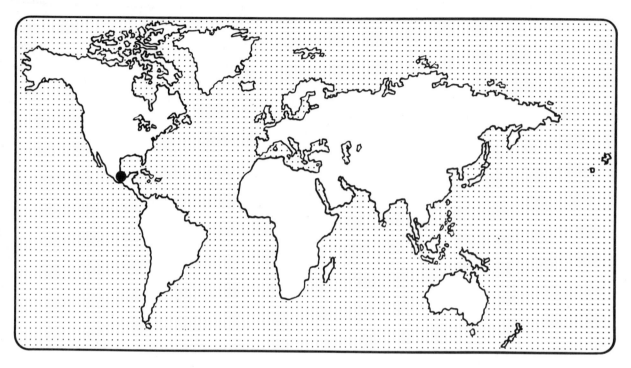

 # GUATEMALA

Cotton had been grown for hundreds of years in Guatemala before the Spanish imported wool. The native crop, which comes in coffee-brown and white, was easier to dye than wool, and in the hot climate more comfortable to wear. Naturally, embroidery was done on cotton backing.

But the conquistadores ruled with a heavy hand. They insisted the people incorporate motifs more familiar to the Spanish. So today we find blends of odd needlework patterns like lions and griffins mixed with ageless designs—dots, lines, spirals, circles.

The Spanish were also strongly opposed to the Mayan practice of human sacrifice. The Maya were Guatemala's great ancient people, who without metal tools, cut stone to make giant ceremonial centers like Tikal. Time was of tremendous interest to the Maya and they devised an astronomical calendar that still amazes scientists with its accuracy. The Spanish were unimpressed. They smashed Mayan idols, burned sacred books, and tore down the pyramids.

On the surface the Indians gave up their Mayan beliefs and converted to Christianity. But when the rains didn't come on schedule in 1975, 400 years after the conquest, the people held secret ceremonies to the Mayan rain god, Chac.

We can learn much from the simplicity of Guatemalan embroidery. First of all, a Guatemalan stitcher is conservative in the use of color, limiting the color scheme to four or five colors. The needleworker uses the same pattern over and over, varying it by changing colors unpredictably to give the impression of more complexity. Aids in embroidering are pure practical genius—no pattern, no rulers, no tracing paper are used. For circular bands of embroidery at the neck the embroiderer pulls the cloth over a basket, ties it tight at the bottom, and swings a needle in an arc from the neck while working to make sure the embroidery is even. A slip of paper is used to measure the spacing between patterns.

Since the embroidery is worked on loosely hand-woven fabric, buttonholes are difficult to make. The fastenings are usually loops or ties, with buttons used decoratively on pockets or edgings. The loose fabric also at times defies embroidery, so the Indians put muslin over the garment, embroider through both fabrics, and cut away the excess muslin. I later remembered this clever trick when I was having difficulty with the Mexican money pouch (section P).

Huipil (long tunic) from Chichicastenango, Guatemala, with taffeta ribbons at neck and shoulders, surrounded by fine chain stitch. The rest of the design is woven, but could be achieved by darning, as in Japanese kogin darning. Collection of the Lowie Museum of Anthropology, University of California, Berkeley.

WORKING PROCESS:
Huipil Embroidery on Tunic

Some of the most striking embroidery in Guatemala is done by the men of Chichicastenango, a place-name that sets the tongue dancing. They face the neckline with black taffeta shaped into long points to symbolize the sun and sewn down with three rows of incredibly fine chain stitch. Once you learn this technique of making a sawtooth edge, you will begin to notice it used large and small in the likes of molas, aprons, and quilts all around the world. The Indians also sew a medallion of ribbon on each shoulder to signify the moon, which affects the success of crops.

We use these techniques in a brightly-colored *huipil* (whee-peel'), the blouse worn by Guatemalan women.

Project Pointers

To avoid holes that show, pin only into the seam allowance of the ribbon.

Use two strands of the six-strand embroidery floss for chain stitch.

YOU WILL NEED

pattern for woman's front-opening tunic (or a ready-made tunic with a long neck opening)
yardage as called for on pattern
1 yard white satin acetate ribbon, 1½" wide (same as for section D, Greece)
1 skein six-strand embroidery floss, white
ruler, pencil, scissors, embroidery needle

1. Preshrink the ribbon when you preshrink the yardage.

2. Cut out the tunic. Sew the front, back, and shoulder seams. It's easier to work if you leave open the underarm and side seams. Cut off ⅜" around the neck edge and front opening; we are using a ¼" seam and do not need the excess. Blow up and transfer the outer four lines of chain stitch from the cartoon to the tunic.

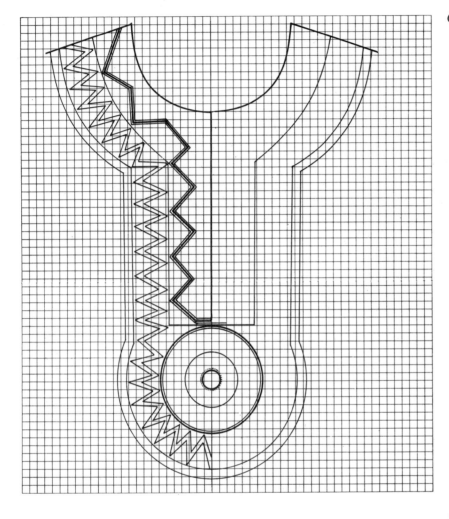

Cartoon   1 square = ¼″

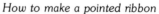

How to make a pointed ribbon

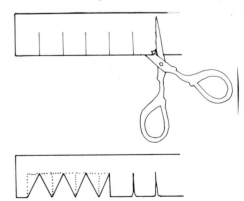

3. Measure the distance from the bottom of the front opening to the neck edge including the neck seam allowance. Add ½″ to the measurement and cut two lengths of ribbon.

4. Press under ½″ on one ribbon. Work on a flat surface to be accurate. With the turned-under edge to your right lay a ruler on the bottom edge of the ribbon. Make a small pencil mark every 1½″ along the length of the ribbon. Now make a cut at each mark ⅝″ into the ribbon. Fold the cut edges toward each other to make a point as shown above and press. Don't worry about stray threads—they'll be covered by embroidery later.

5. Repeat step 4 on the second length of ribbon except start with the turned-under edge to your left.

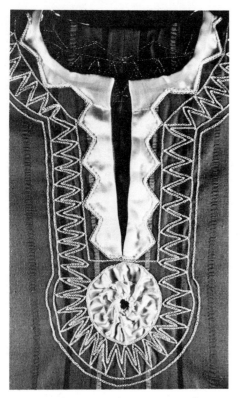

Project photo

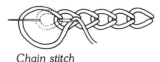

Chain stitch

6. From now on do not pin into the ribbon except within the seam allowance, as the holes will show. Along the front opening match the right side of the ribbons to the wrong side of the tunic with the uncut edge of the ribbons along the raw edges of the fabric. The turned-under edge of the ribbons should fall *exactly* at the bottom of the front opening. Stitch a ¼″ seam by hand or machine on each side of the front opening. Turn the ribbons to the outside and press into place. I had extra time so I basted the ribbons in place along the outside edge, but this is optional.

7. Measure the tunic's neck edge, add 1″, and cut this length of ribbon. Press both ends in ½″. Fold the two ends together and press lightly to find the center back.

8. Measure, mark, cut, and press every 1½″ as in step 4 above, but work from both ends toward the middle. Change the angle of the middle back point to fit as needed.

9. Pin right side of ribbon to wrong side of neck edge, matching front edges and center back. Stitch ¼″ seam, turn to outside, and press. Overcast the front edges where the ribbons overlap.

10. Using two strands of the six-strand embroidery floss, chain stitch along the edge of the ribbon all around the neck and down the front edge. Do a second row of stitching on the tunic snuggled up against the edge of the ribbon.

11. For the circle cut a piece of ribbon 8½″ long. Sew the ends with a ¼″ seam. Run long basting stitches along one edge of the ribbon. Pull the stitches up tight so the ribbon forms a circle. Lay it in place on the tunic and baste it in place. Stitch one row of chain stitch around the outside edge of the ribbon. Stitch another row of chain stitch halfway in on the ribbon.

12. Stitch the remaining four lines of chain stitch.

ADDITIONAL IDEAS

1. Combine the Guatemalan ribbon edge with the West African design (section M) for a caftan.
2. Use the Egyptian collar pattern and colors (section C), but work a row of small colored ribbon circles appliquéd where the teardrops and circles fall, surrounded by rows of chain stitch.
3. Edge a quilt with a larger version of the ribbon edge.

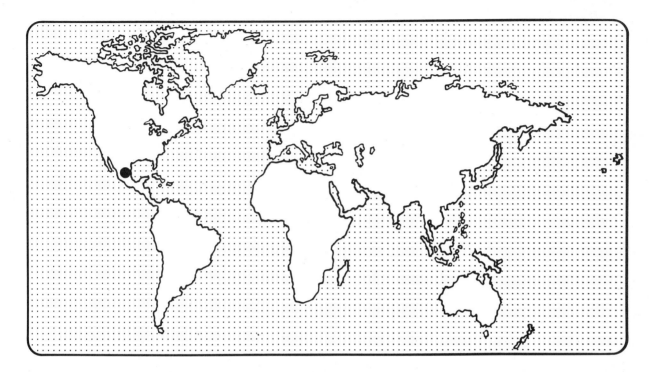

MEXICO

Cross stitch is found anywhere in the world that fabric can be hand-woven using the same thread for warp and weft. This produces an even-weave fabric that lends itself to embroidery worked over a certain number of threads. These counted-thread designs tend to be geometric. Although similar motifs like the double-headed eagle and the eight-pointed star pop up all over the world, each country produces its own delightful variety of designs.

For example, in many different areas of Mexico cross stitch is worked on a hand-woven cotton fabric. The Huichol Indian men in west-central Mexico wear a string of little cross-stitched bags around their waists. With no openings, these bags are purely decorative and serve only to make the wearer feel special and the viewer feel happy. Larger bags are also made, and these do have openings for carrying money and other valuables. Many of the designs on the larger bags are deliberately off-center, which, to me, makes the embroiderer seem more human.

The combination of European and Indian motifs in embroidery

comes from Mexico's rich history of strong people and stronger conquerors. Long ago in central Mexico the Aztecs ruled with a benevolent but stern hand. Like the Mayans in Guatemala, they erected massive temples without the use of metal tools or beasts of burden like donkeys or horses.

They did know how to fashion gold and semiprecious stones into jewelry and the riches of this art attracted the Spanish. In 1519 Hernando Cortes landed on the Gulf of Mexico and for the next 300 years, the Spanish ruled the Aztecs. Many Aztec traditions were not allowed under this reign, but even with the European motifs forced on the Mexicans, the Indian art remained alive.

Mexican colors are gay reds, oranges, pinks, blues, and greens, often set off by white fabric. What strikes you immediately is how a small bit of embroidered color transforms a simple costume into something memorable. This surprising and effective use of simple accent goes a long way towards explaining today's burgeoning interest in collecting Mexican folk needlework.

Speaking of collecting, with so many new major roads opening in Mexico, access to the crafts of mountain Indians will be easier. As in all parts of the world, the makers will continue to produce in quantity whatever sells. If you set a personal standard of only buying well-made embroidery in your travels, perhaps quality will not fade in Mexico (or anywhere else in the world).

Of course you will rarely be able to buy traditional folk embroidery. This is carefully passed from mother to daughter, father to son, carrying on the symbols meaningful to each community in embroidered clothing and household furnishing. Being folk art, it is meant to be used personally, not mass-produced.

Huichol cross-stitched bags, from collection of the Lowie Museum of Anthropology, University of California, Berkeley

How We Made Computer Designs

Each pattern in this box, as well as those on the Mexican money bag, was created by a computer. The computer was programmed with rules from a game called "Life." These rules are a simple version of the way living things grow from generation to generation. Each pattern is a generation of x's, and the next generation grows from it. X's either *die* if they get too crowded or isolated, *grow* new x's if they have enough room, or just *remain* (like the central four in the later generations).

The amazing thing is how much these computer-generated patterns are like traditional cross stitch ones. Maybe though, it's not that surprising: these computer patterns grew "organically," just as the folk designs did.

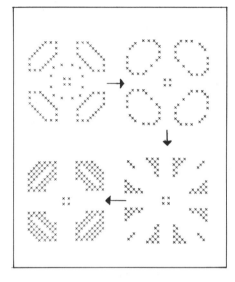

Stitch diagram

WORKING PROCESS:
Cross Stitch Money Bag

We've adapted the Huichol bags for use as a money pouch or key-holder that can be fastened to the arm or leg of a hiker, runner, or biker. The cross stitch design, remarkably similar to traditional Mexican designs, was actually generated by a computer.

YOU WILL NEED

4½" × 7" piece of even-weave fabric, 14 threads/inch (or use #14 mono canvas as waste canvas on any fabric)
4½" × 7× lining material (optional)
14–17" grosgrain ribbon
3–4" Velcro (or other nylon snap) tape or three Velcro buttons
1 skein each, six-strand embroidery floss: red, blue, and light blue
tapestry needle, scissors
doodle cloth

Project photo

Project Pointers

If your fabric is too loosely woven for cross stitch, back it with a finely woven fabric like batiste.
Cross all stitches the same way.
Each color symbol on the graph stands for one complete cross stitch.

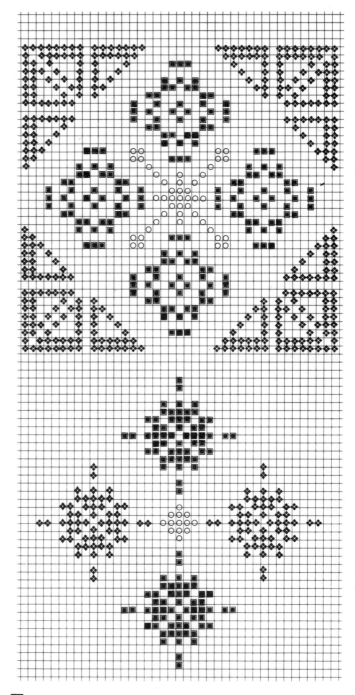

■ = Red

❖ = Dark Blue

○ = Light Blue

1. Tape edges of the piece of even-weave fabric if it ravels. Back it with the lining material (I used batiste), if your cross stitches slip between the threads. (Practice on the doodle cloth to check it.) Fold the 7" edge in half to find the centerfold and baste a thread along it. Then find the halfway point both vertically and horizontally on each of the two halves. It is a cross of two threads, not a center hole. Mark with pencil dots.

2. Use two strands of the six-strand embroidery floss. Follow the color code on the cartoon and be sure to cross all the stitches the same way. You can start anywhere, but I found it easiest to work from the center out. The first time you work a pattern, it's slow counting stitches, but soon you are greeting each repeat like an old friend.

3. Whether or not you work the back half of the bag is optional. It is not visible while being worn. I'm a fanatic; I worked it.

4. When done with the embroidery, remove the tape and trim the lining close to the stitching. Fold the ribbon in half to find the halfway point. Match it to the vertical center of the front. Lay the bottom edge of the ribbon four threads away from the last row of cross stitches. Stitch in place by hand or machine.

5. Turn under both ends of the bag three threads from the last row of cross stitches. Stitch a row of buttonhole stitches two threads high along both ends of the bag. Sew a Velcro button or ½" of Velcro tape to both sides inside the bag.

6. Fold the bag in half along the line you basted. Stitch by hand or machine along both sides three threads from the embroidery. Remove the basting thread. Unravel the vertical threads on the edges to make a small fringe.

7. Measure the bag on the arm, thigh, or ankle of its owner. Cut the ribbon shorter if necessary. Stitch the remaining Velcro tape or buttons onto the ends of the ribbon.

Cross stitch

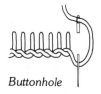

Buttonhole

ADDITIONAL IDEAS

1. Use this pattern in the dollhouse rug of section R, Russia. Repeat the dark blue border on the back half design.
2. Work a sewing tote in these cross stitch blocks, repeated to fill the entire space.
3. Adapt parts of the Bulgarian darning pattern to this little bag. It makes a great present.

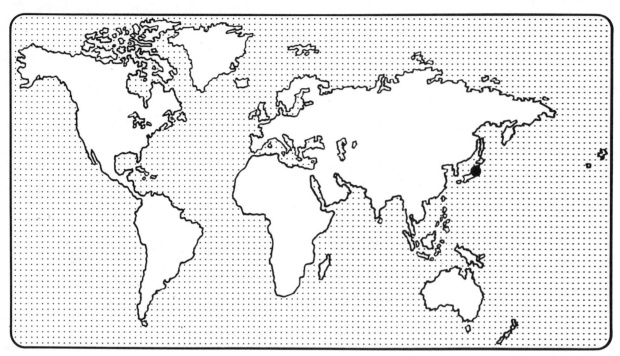

 # JAPAN

"**N**othing's sure but death and taxes" is as timeless as ethnic embroidery. Two hundred years ago Japan was ruled by military governors, the shoguns, who claimed almost all the crops and anything of minor value in taxation. The farmers on the northern end of Japan's main island of Honshu were left practically nothing but the coats on their backs. But like people round the world since the day of skins, the farmers brought simple beauty to a simple covering through simple embroidery.

The kogin (ko-geen'), a short jacket worn by Japanese farmers, both male and female, was originally woven from wild karamushi, a natural grass similar to hemp. Since farmers in Japan carry poles and baskets across their shoulders, the first embroidery was simple running stitches on the yoke of the kogin, designed to strengthen the fabric. Before long an observant needleworker realized that staggering the stitches would produce a pleasing pattern, and kogin darning was born.

Soon the military governor, or shogun, of the island of Honshu, where the work originated, noticed the new beauty of the kogin. The embroidery was originally worked with dark blue thread on dark blue fabric. In 1788 a more benevolent shogun allowed the peasant class to use white cotton thread for the embroidery. He also developed the overall form for the placement of the patterns and with minor variations, this form is still followed. The yoke is worked in groupings of three rows of running stitch, making it appear striped. The top narrow pattern across the two sides of the front often includes a hex symbol to protect the wearer from evil. Another narrow band of pattern follows, and then large areas of pattern are stitched on the side fronts and back.

On many kogin each area, left and right, has a different pattern, which was a subtle way for the embroiderer to show off skill and knowledge of patterns. Each area has a descriptive name like "cat's claw," "upside-down fist," and "wood grain eaten by bugs."

The Japanese loom is narrow, so yardage is only about 14″ wide. These costumes are ingeniously fashioned from four lengths of yardage plus some sleeves (see illustration) and can easily be adapted to modern materials. For Sunday wear a farmer would make a kogin with fuller sleeves and a velvet or satin collar. Children were taught weaving at age five by beginning with five warps (the up-and-down threads you weave across). Every other year two warp threads were added until the child could handle a full loom. (Wouldn't this be a simple way for an adult to learn weaving?)

WORKING PROCESS:
Kogin Darning on Camera or Guitar Strap

Some of the best cameras in the world are made in Japan today. It seems appropriate to adapt a traditional Japanese pattern for a camera (or guitar) strap. We reversed the traditional white thread on blue fabric, using blue thread on white linen.

Project Pointers

Replace the neck part of your camera strap with kogin darning.
Don't pull the stitches tight or the strap linen will ripple.

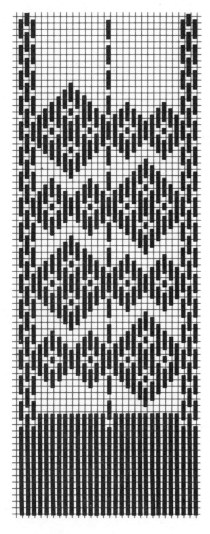

Stitch diagram

Project photo

YOU WILL NEED

2 skeins #5 pearl cotton, navy blue
1⅛ yards strap linen (2⅜" wide, 20 threads/inch) or ⅛ yard any
    even-weave fabric
⅛ yard lining
adjustable camera strap
doodle cloth (cut off 4" of the strap linen)

1. Practice a running stitch on your doodle cloth, stitching over three threads and under one. Don't pull too tight or the fabric will ripple.

2. Cut the strap linen 3" longer than the neck strap on your camera.

3. This is a fast and easy pattern that's fun to work. Fold the strap linen in half lengthwise to find the center holes. Mark with a pin. Working from right to left the length of the strap linen, begin with a waste knot on top and come out about 1" from the end of the center line. It is not necessary to work right to the ends as these will be folded under in finishing. Work the center line, over three threads, under one.

4. Now count out 14 holes from either side of the center line. Mark each with a pin. Stitch a line identical to the center line, making certain the running stitches are lined up on all three lines.

5. Twelve holes from either side of the center are two more identical lines of running stitch.

6. Between the outer rows of running stitch is a row of staggered stitches. Look at the cartoon for the placement of this row.

7. From now on your work is easy. Each line of stitches is repeated four times, two on each side of the center line. Stitch all four lines of each stitch sequence before going on to the next sequence. At the end of each line check your stitching—to make a mistake and not notice it would be gruesome. And don't forget to look at the back of your work—it's the negative of the front.

8. Either turn under the edges of your strap and stitch it directly to the leather neck strap; or stitch the lining to the strap linen, right sides together. Measure the darned strap to neck strap; cut off excess at ends, leaving ½". It's easiest to leave an opening for turning halfway down the long side. Clip corners and waste knots left on the ends. Turn, press, and slip stitch opening closed.

Kogin darning on kimono, from the island of Honshu, Japan. Photo courtesy of Royal Ontario Museum.

ADDITIONAL IDEAS

1. Use this pattern in white on the side of navy placements.
2. Turn the pattern sideways on the strap linen. Work a set of three patterns *across* the linen, not lengthwise, in one color from the Bulgarian design (section F, p. 64). Work the next set of patterns in a different color. Make a belt.
3. Work the front yoke of a caftan in this pattern, either using even-weave fabric or basting waste canvas onto white fabric. Construct the main part of the caftan from patterned blue-and-white fabric.

SUPPLIES AND BIBLIOGRAPHY—COTTON

Dewey Decimal library call numbers given in parentheses when known

Cotton

Crawford, M.D.C. *The Heritage of Cotton.* New York: Fairchild, 1948.

National Cotton Council of America, P.O. Box 12285, Memphis, TN 38112.

Whaley's Fabrics, 118 N. Main St., Sebastopol, CA 95472—100% cotton fabrics, $1 for bag of swatches.

India

Design in Indian Textiles. Indian Institute of Art on Industry, Calcutta, 1963.

Dongerkery, Kamala S. *The Romance of Indian Embroidery.* Bombay: Thacker and Co., 1951.

Nanavati, J. M. *The Embroidery and Bead Work of Kutch and Saurashtra.* Department of Archaeology, Gujarat State, India, 1966.

Textiles and Embroideries of India. Bombay: Marg Publications.

Textiles and Ornaments of India. The Museum of Modern Art, New York, 1956.

Kitsophrenia, Inc., Box 5042, Glendale, CA 91210—shisha mirrors.

Gambia

Aronson, Lisa. "The Designing Women of West Africa." *Natural History,* January 1975.

Dendel, Esther Warner. *African Fabric Crafts.* New York: Taplinger, 1974. $10.95 (746).

Jeffers, Louise E. *The Decorative Arts of Africa.* New York: Viking Press, 1973.

Newman, Thelma. *Contemporary African Arts and Crafts.* Crown. $7.95 (745).

Panama

Auld, Rhoda L. *Molas.* New York: Van Nostrand Reinhold, 1977. $13.50 (746.4).

Discovery. Magazine of the Peabody Museum of Natural History. New Haven: Yale University, spring 1973—several articles on the Cuna People.

Salvador, Mari Lyn. "The Clothing Arts of the Cuna of San Blas, Panama." In *Ethnic and Tourist Arts,* edited by Nelson H. H.

Graburn. Berkeley: University of California Press, 1976. $19.95 (709E).

Guatemala

O'Neale, Lila M. *Textiles of Highland Guatemala.* Carnegie Institute of Washington, DC, 1945.

"The Maya, The Children of Time." *National Geographic,* December 1975.

Mexico

Goodman, Frances Schaill. *The Embroidery of Mexico and Guatemala.* New York: Scribner's, 1976. $14.95 (746.4G).

Num, Alejandro Dumas. *La Familia.* 107 (Esq. Presidente Masaryk) Mexico 5, DF—monthly women's magazine with many needlework patterns.

Japan

Musterberg, Hugo. *Mingei: Folk Arts of Old Japan.* The Asia Society, New York.

Tomoyuki Yamanobe, *Japanese Textiles.* Rutland, VT: Charles E. Tuttle, 1957.

Tsugaru-Kogin. Japan Vogue. $4.70.

Japan Publications Trading Co., Inc., 200 Clearbrook Rd, Elmsford, NY 10523—many beautiful embroidery books, charted but not translated.

Yvonne Porcella combines fabrics from Guatemala with molas, ribbons, and a mirror purse from Pakistan in an original ethnic dress. Photo courtesy of the artist.

139

part four 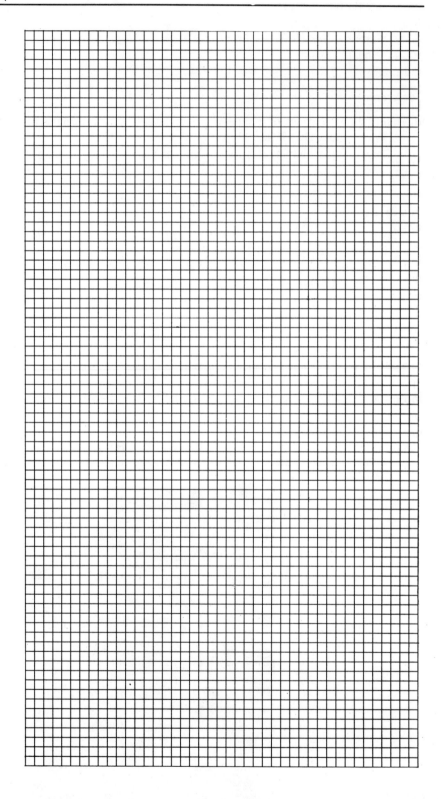 WOOL

It's the end of the Stone Age. Imagine that you live in the meadow (outside your nonexistent twentieth-century village) with a few neighbors and a flock of sheep. You do not know any farming techniques, so finding food is always a problem, especially with the birth of more and more people. Fortunately, in the meadow the weather is kind and it stays about 70° all year long.

This is not true in the tall mountains that ring the meadow. Five minutes into them and a person begins to freeze, so the children are forbidden to go near them. Every night around the campfire you all sing songs of thanks for the temperate climate.

But the elders in your group worry about the shrinking environment—more people, same space, less food. You, being the acknowledged smart one, are sent out to do the Environmental Impact Study on the meadow. As you walk you notice that bits of fleece from the sheep have caught on bushes. You pluck off a ball of this wool and absent-mindedly roll it in your hand as you explore the meadow. The wool is soft and fluffy and filthy, with dirt and seeds caught in it. The grease feels soothing to your rough hands. "Why haven't I ever noticed this before?" you wonder.

The sheep are milling around the lake in their favorite spot as you approach and you marvel at all that fluffy fleece. Butting and bumping each other, they run from you. You look down at the dirty wool on the ground, matted together by sheep hooves. Holding your nose, you pick up the mat and wash it in the cold lake. It doesn't look so bad, cleaned up.

While it's drying on a bush, you take a nap. You have a dream in which you've come up with an ingenious solution to your community's problem and you see yourself being congratulated all over the campground. But what's this? There you are, leading everybody into the mountains. Are you crazy? Nobody goes into the mountains.

You sit up fast, shivering. A cold breeze is blowing off the lake. You curse yourself for not bringing your jackrabbit pelt for warmth. "Oh why not," you think, putting the warm wool mat over your shoulders. "They'll all laugh at me back at camp, but I can throw it away before I get there."

What kind of person are *you?* Would you have thrown this crude felt away when you got home, or would you have noticed how warm it is—warm enough in fact, to get you comfortably over the mountains into new lands, new climates. As long as you took your sheep with you, you would have had a source of warmth that set you free of one locale.

The first use of wool as a fiber—as distinct from sheepskin as a "fur"—was probably this primitive felt. Much later (wo)man learned to spin the wool fleece and weave it into even warmer coverings. Other people wanted this naturally air-conditioned fabric and early interregional trade was based on wool. Woolen items were made as early as 4000 B.C. in Mesopotamia, but it is not known exactly where the first spinning took place. Since wool is a protein, it is subject to decomposition in warm, damp climates. The oldest dated fabric is a scrap of felt found by James Mellaart in Chinese Turkestan, dating back to 6000 B.C.

Early sheep probably had black fleece, not the off-white we see today. In the Bible Isaac is documented as the first scientific breeder. He knew that the Oriental way of cross-breeding goats with sheep was not good for either. The animals did not live long, and the fleece remained black. He began separating the two flocks, and this was the beginning of the symbolism of lambs as innocent and goats as evil. It was also the beginning of new colors in sheep fleece, which slowly changed from black to brown to gray, but even a few years ago mothers were still singing "Baa, baa, black sheep" to sleepy kids.

Sheep and wool spread to Europe overland through Greece, although legend has it that the first sheep in England were brought by Phoenician ships (that must have been an aromatic trip). At any rate, sheep were available in England as early as 50 A.D. for the Roman conquerors to set up a woolens factory. By the thirteenth century, England was the center of the wool trade and her history was interwoven with wool thereafter.

During the reign of Henry VIII, the king seized flocks belonging to monasteries and gave them to his friends, who fenced them in. This raised the unemployment rate among shepherds, who soon found themselves in debtors' prisons. As a result many immigrated to the new American colonies.

England was not happy with the idea of wool competition and discouraged the export of sheep to America. Nevertheless, sheep were smuggled in, and considerable trade in wool fabrics quickly developed. In fact, the charter of Massachusetts was revoked by England in 1684 for violation of the Navigation Acts—in other words, Americans had their hands slapped for trading wool. Actually, it was worse than a hand slap. By the late 1600's England had made sheep and wool trading an offense punishable by cutting off the criminal's right hand. Wearing wool fabrics became a political act, a visible symbol of revolution. Both George Washington and Thomas Jefferson were inaugurated in American wool suits.

Later Merino sheep were imported from Spain to improve the

quality of American wool. Merino is the Rolls Royce of wool—fine, soft, high quality. Our major source of Merino wool today is Australia, which is amazing considering the fact that their entire industry is descended from 13 Merino rams sold in 1797 by one British commander to another British officer who had settled in Australia.

Some Types of Wool*

Fabrics: felt—now usually made partly of man-made fibers, flannel, gabardine, jersey, serge, sharkskin, worsted, tweed

Threads: French wool, crewel, Persian wool (a 3-ply wool sold by single *strand* or in a *hank*), bouclé, knitting, rug, handspun

*Note: Of course the term *wool* refers to more animals than sheep—such as camel, goat (cashmere and mohair), llama, vicuna, alpaca. Both luxury fabrics and threads of these animals, can be found by diligent searching. But in general, when we say "wool," we mean sheep wool.

SEWING ON AND WITH WOOL

Wool fabric is usually preshrunk—check the bolt or your fabric dealer for information. Sewing on wool is a pleasure. It handles beautifully and with proper care retains its shape over the years. Use a ballpoint needle and be sure to press (not iron) with steam and a presscloth. When sewing on single or double-knit wools, use sewing tape in the shoulder seams, waistlines, and necklines to keep the fabric from stretching. If you are allergic to the dye or finish on wool, totally line your garments.

Working with wool threads is a similar joy. Because wool dyes so easily, the color range is spectacular. Before stitching with wool, close your eyes and run your thumb and forefinger lightly down and up the strand. There is a right and wrong way to wool yarn, just as there is to your hair. When you decide which way is right, thread the top of the yarn into the needle. Then as the thread is pulled through the fabric, the scales will be smoothed instead of roughed up. If you are working with stranded wool, separate it into single strands before recombining it. This prevents the yarn from bumping up on the surface.

CARE OF WOOL

The outstanding characteristic of wool is that it springs back to its original shape, making it wrinkle-resistant. Take advantage of this by hanging up garments on padded, shaped hangers or pants hangers. Unbutton a tight coat if you must sit in it a period of time. An easy way to refresh wool while traveling is to hang it in the bathroom while you take a shower.

Some wools are now machine-washable and -dryable but most must be dry-cleaned. Blot up spots immediately with a damp cloth. Use the soft brush attachment of your vacuum cleaner to remove embedded dirt and lint.

It is extremely important in needlepoint to use a reliable marker on your backing fabric that will not run into the wool when you block your piece. Check with your favorite yarn store to be sure, or test a small piece of canvas by marking and wetting it.

Counted thread work by Jody House, wool and pearl cotton on needlepoint canvas—yellows, purples, greens mounted on green felt.

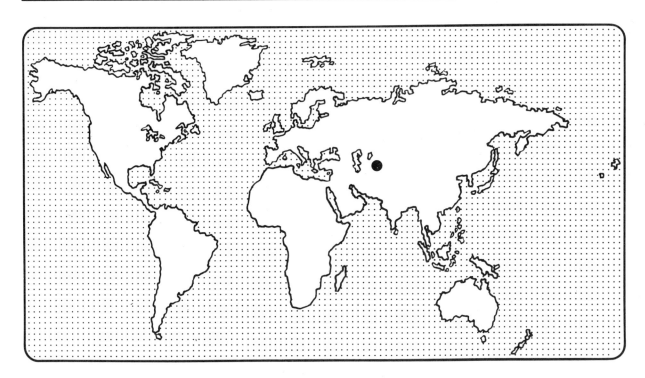

RUSSIA

The life of a nomad calls for portable objects, and so the embroidery on each piece is usually very elaborate. It's like the quilts made by U.S. pioneer women as they crossed the country—the necessary quilting was usually finished before journey's end, so the needleworkers spent the rest of the trip quilting elaborate designs into every square inch of material.

Similarly, the embroidery of the Uzbek nomads, a Turkoman tribe, lifted simple cross and chain stitch with silk thread to a fine art. Exposure to many cultures, including Persian, Indian, and Chinese, influenced the designs of the nomads, and so we find those in the west to be naturalistic floral patterns similar to Indian prints or crewel embroidery, while those in the east are filled with moons, stars, and esoteric symbols. In interpreting these symbols textile historians can be misguided. For example, one tribe's use of circles in embroidery was declared a sign of sun worship . . . until the nomads revealed that the pattern was originally known as "Forty Moons." These symbols evolved in many different cultures, and for an outsider to pretend to understand them is folly. (To find the area where the Uzbeks live, look in your atlas for Tashkent, in southwestern Russia, north of Afghanistan.)

Among the Uzbeks, the original purpose of a dowry was to pass down those symbols magical to a family. Not only would they protect the newlyweds from harm, but the tribal emblems would never die out. Soon the dowry items were worth money, and as outsiders collected them, the more mystifying designs changed to appeal to a wider audience.

This also changed the social order. Before, women had embroidered for the home; now men began staying home and embroidering.

The nomads had many tricks to make embroidering possible on long trips. One person, usually an elder woman, drew the design on six or seven long strips. Everyone embroidered one, and then they sewed them all together. In your own work, breaking a design down into modules, as we did on this project, means you can work on the go. Another idea comes from the nomadic practice of removing embroidery from ankles of trousers and garments for washing. Design your own pop-out embroidery to snap into a bodice or to wrap around a wrist with nylon snap tape.

Project photo

WORKING PROCESS:
Uzbek Embroidery Dollhouse Rug

Rugs have always been important to nomadic people, and archeological findings show that felt rugs were used long before knotted or woven ones. We have borrowed a typical Uzbek ram's horn pattern and changed it for a needlepoint rug to brighten a dollhouse. The same motif, by the way, appears in other places around the world under different names. In Turkey it's called the "Dragonfoot."

Project Pointers

Each color symbol on the cartoon stands for one half-cross stitch.

Don't pull the center stitches tight or the canvas will bump up.

Color Code

■ = Red

○ = Yellow

◉ = Blue

■ = Black

□ = White

Unmarked = Gold

Stitch diagram

YOU WILL NEED

7½" × 4" piece of #14 canvas
1 skein, #5 pearl cotton, black
1 hank each, French or 3-ply Persian wool: red, white, gold
4 strands each, French or Persian wool: blue, yellow
19" brown purchased fringe, 1" wide
tapestry needle, scissors
doodle cloth

Half-cross stitch—work it right to left

1. Turn under ½" on all edges of the canvas and baste into place. Cut away excess at the corners. Find the halfway point of the long edge and baste a thread across it. Find the center points of both halves; the center point will be two threads crossing, not a hole. Mark with pencil dots.

2. Practice on a doodle cloth to see how many piles of the Persian wool to use. I used one ply of the 3-ply white, two plies of the French, and all other colors of Persian wool.

3. Each unit of the two-unit design is worked in quarters, rotating the canvas. Use a half-cross stitch for everything but the black lines, which are cross stitch. Begin at the center of one unit. Stitch as shown above in white. Then rotate the canvas one-quarter turn, and stitch another small white triangle. Don't pull the stitches tight, or the center will bump up. Continue stitching each color in quarters, keeping the center to your upper left as you stitch.

4. Everything is symmetrical *except* the blue side lines. Count carefully from the cartoon.

5. As you stitch at the edges, go through both layers of canvas as if they were one. Now you won't need to finish the edges.

6. When finished, put the rug face-down on a towel and steam-press it. It should need no further blocking.

7. Sew the fringe to the outside edge by tiny overcast stitches.

ADDITIONAL IDEAS

1. Fold the units in half and stitch up the sides into a money bag as in section P, Mexico, p. 129).
2. Repeat this unit in latch hooking on rug canvas.
3. The Uzbek work that inspired this design was done in tiny silk cross stitches. Do likewise across the band of a silk evening halter.

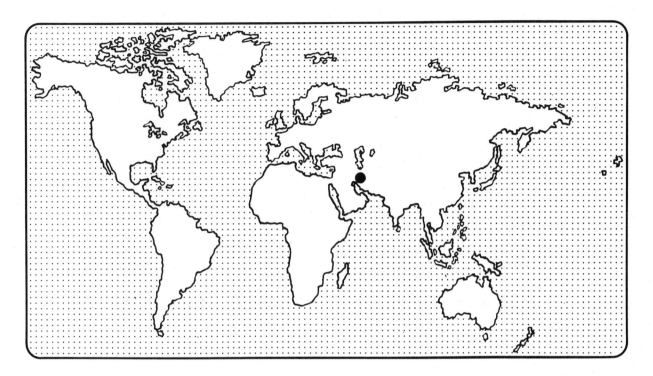

PERSIA (IRAN)

In 1971 the Shah of Iran celebated the 2500th anniversary of the founding of the Persian empire by Cyrus the Great. This long history of Persia has been dominated by two elements: invasion and love of art. It is said that as soon as the basic needs of hunger and shelter are met, a Persian buys or makes art. Art truly belongs to all, from the poorest to the richest, and is not considered a luxury, but a part of life.

Consider the ways that Persian art is and has been encouraged to blend with society, and compare it to our lives: first, people look to the artists to convey the sacred and ancient knowledge of the way life works; second, there has always been royal patronage; third, the ancient techniques and themes are constantly updated for contemporary needs; and last, the artists do not work alone but are organized into studios and workshops.

The master craftspeople of these studios are highly respected. Perhaps it is because the creation of beauty is considered a step closer to God that standards in crafts are so high. If the work is to be

Resht work with inlaid appliqué embroidery on wool broadcloth. Photo courtesy of Royal Ontario Museum.

judged by God and not your neighbor, you would go to the trouble of working a delicate filigree *under* a silver inlay—work that will never be seen unless the water jug it's on is broken.

In a desert land of scorching sun the height of luxury is a shady garden with running water. These classic gardens are immortalized in the famous Persian rugs, where each flower, tree, and color has a symbolic meaning (green = justice, red = valor, yellow = jealousy, for example). Those educated in the meanings of the symbols can "read" a Persian rug.

Resht, in the northwest by the Caspian Sea, is the center of several groups of nomadic people descended from the same Turkoman tribes we mentioned in the last section. These people decorate their tents, horses, and camels lavishly with embroidery. One major item of furniture is a richly embroidered carpet bag. On the move it holds goods; in the tent you sit or lean on it. A distinctive form of patchwork is done by these tribes, with red and green flannel mounted on cotton print and emphasized by stitchery on the seams. Below hang little diamond shapes, separately bound by bias tape and attached to each other by beads or buttons, blue to scare away the "evil eye."

The embroiderer, often a man, holds the fabric in a wooden clamp that looks like a giant stapler. The open end grasps the cloth and the other end is tucked under the worker's leg. This allows the fabric to be held taut or loose as needed and enables the embroiderer to do stitches that don't work easily in a frame.

WORKING PROCESS:
Resht Embroidery Backpack *See also color plates 1 and 2*

Like the nomadic tribes, we like to decorate our traveling bags. If this backpack seems too elegant for the mountains, consider wearing it to your next party, leaving your hands free for whatever. The design was adapted from an old Persian textile printing block.

Project Pointers

In free machine embroidery back the fabric with typing-weight scrap paper to prevent puckering.

YOU WILL NEED

⅞ yard medium to heavy yellow material

1 yard webbing for straps, 1½″ wide

1 skein each, #5 pearl cotton: light and dark orange, red, magenta, yellow, light and dark purple

1 spool each, 100% cotton or 100% polyester sewing machine thread: green and blue-green

6″ × 12″ piece medium-weight blue fabric

6″ × 12″ piece iron-on interfacing

1 package single-fold bias tape, orange

embroidery needle, hoop, scissors

sewing machine

1 spool each, sewing machine thread: yellow and orange

typing-weight scrap paper

doodle cloth

Project photo and detail

1. Cut yellow fabric as shown above. Transfer the design to one of the 11½″ × 15″ rectangles, flipping the cartoon over for the left side of the pattern. Don't waste your time copying the leafy part of the paisley, as it will be worked separately on blue fabric.

Color Code

G = Green

O = Orange

Y = Yellow

R = Red

V = Violet

LV = Light Violet (Lavender)

M = Magenta

T = Tangerine

BG = Bright Green

1 square = ¼″

Backpack layout

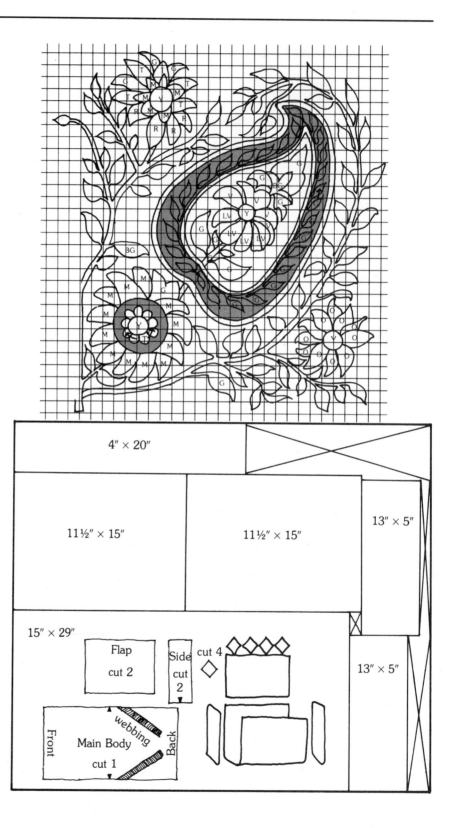

2. Practice free machine embroidery on your doodle cloth, using the hoop. See Africa, section M, steps 4 and 5 (p.116), for how to set up your machine. Use the 100% cotton or 100% polyester thread on top and in the bobbin. Loosen top tension slightly. To make each leaf, stitch back and forth until the shape is filled in.

3. Fill in all the green and blue-green leafy areas in free machine straight stitch. Put typing-weight scrap paper behind your fabric to keep it from puckering. When you are done with all the machine work, tear off the excess paper. Move the hoop as you progress.

4. Using a hoop and the embroidery needle, satin stitch all the flowers in colors as shown on the cartoon. I stitched at an angle across each petal. Begin and end with small backstitches in the flower center, which will later be covered by the yellow satin stitch. This part is slow, so don't hurry—listen to Jacques Brel, talk to your family, enjoy.

5. Transfer the paisley and its leaves to the blue fabric, remembering to flip the paisley over for the left side. I used a white pencil to draw on the blue fabric. Two of the flowers have blue centers. Transfer these two circles and their tiny cartoons for yellow and orange satin stitches.

6. Iron iron-on interfacing to the back of the blue fabric.

7. Mount the blue fabric in the hoop and free machine the green leaves.

8. Reverse the hoop for hand embroidery and satin stitch the two circles as shown on the cartoon.

9. Cut out the two paisleys. Cut out their centers. Cut out the two circles.

10. Pin the paisleys in place, following the cartoon. Lay yellow pearl cotton along the inner and outer edges of the paisleys. Couch by hand or machine.

11. Pin the circles in place. Lay magenta pearl cotton around the edges and couch by hand or machine. I did such a lousy job by machine that I had to add a row of backstitches to hide the yellow fabric peeking through.

12. Now you know enough to embroider the four diamonds. Do so, on the 4″ × 20″ piece of fabric, leaving 1″ between diamonds. Each is 2⅛″ square.

13. Lay the second 11½″ × 15″ rectangle on top of the embroi-

dered flap. Stitch around the sides and bottom with a ½" seam. Clip corners, turn, and press.

14. Cut the webbing into two 18" straps. Lay them inward from the two sides of the back 2½" above the cuts. Pin in place.
15. Lay one side strip on the main body over the straps. Match the notch on one side strip to the notch on the side of the main body. Using a ½" seam, stitch from the notch to ½" from the corner. Leave the needle in the fabric and raise the presser bar lever. Clip from the corner in so you can make the main body turn the corner. Continue to stitch up the side. Then stitch from the center notch up the other side, handling the turn at the corner in the same way.

16. Repeat step 15 for the second side. Turn right side out and press.

17. Match the outside of the upper back to the open edge of the embroidered flap and lining. Stitch a ½" seam.

18. Turn under and press ¼" on the top of the backpack. Turn another ¼" and topstitch.

19. Try on the pack. Bring the webbing straps under your arms and over your shoulders until you find a comfortable length. Stitch securely to the back of the pack.

20. Cut out the four diamonds. Cut out four undecorated diamonds. Place the two groups, decorated and undecorated, wrong sides together. Stitch orange bias tape around the edge of each diamond. Overlap the points of adjoining diamonds and hand stitch them together. Hand stitch the diamonds to the flap.

ADDITIONAL IDEAS

1. Work this design on white organza curtains in shadow appliqué and shadow stitching (but read section Y, Portugal, p. 182, first).
2. Work a series of diamonds, and appliqué them to the bottom of a long evening dress.
3. Satin stitch the orange-and-yellow centers of the two main flowers on the centers of the paisleys that you cut out of blue fabric. Line with a stiff interlining like buckram. Buttonhole the two paisleys together, leaving an opening for your embroidery scissors. Buttonhole the two free edges (separately, not together).

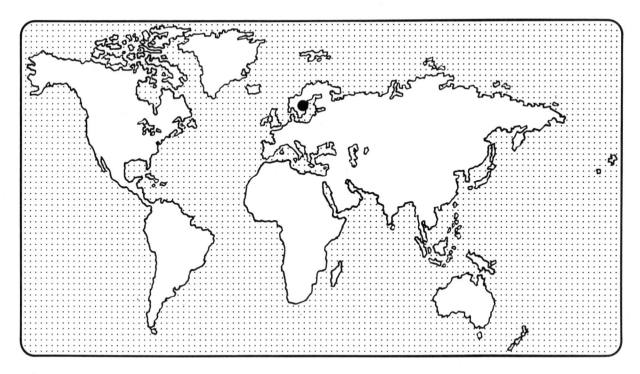

SWEDEN

Many modern American needleworkers got their start in embroidery by falling in love with the Swedish kits so readily available. There is a distinctive look to Swedish work that makes it immediately identifiable—simple yet colorful, rhythmic, and balanced— and more importantly, it inspires you to pick up a needle and begin stitching.

For hundreds of years, every item in the typical Swedish home was hand-made and hand-embellished. The men even took the trouble to paint or carve the tools they used in the fields. The prestige of early homes was elevated by the number of fine fabrics and embroideries that could be displayed for celebrations. Every chair and bench had a special cushion, with the best on the seat of honor. Hangings covered all walls and rafters right up to the ridgepole. If there were bare spots, they were quickly covered by paintings on paper or bedsheets.

For very festive dinners a big cloth was suspended over the table like a canopy. The four corners were fastened to rings in the rafters and red apples hung down from each corner. The center was caught up with a crown made of straw. (This inspired me to make a similar spur-of-the-moment canopy out of a printed bed sheet for a family friend who was coming to dinner. He was amused that we added this small but special touch just for him and didn't tease me much when the sheet drooped down on us between soup and salad.)

Incidentally, the well-known rya rugs from Sweden were originally not for the floor, but were bed coverings used with the pile side down. Carpets and curtains were unknown in early houses. For special occasions the floor was sprinkled with chopped-fir twigs.

Both wool and linen were hand-spun and hand-woven in the home. A young Swedish girl would begin embroidering a linen shirt for her betrothed long before she knew exactly whom she'd marry—consequently she made it large and billowy so it would fit anyone.

Extending north over 12° of latitude, Sweden has an amazing variety in climate, soil, and plant life. This of course is reflected in any hand-dyed yarns used in needlework—thus brightly colored yarns are used in one area, pastels in another. Halsingland is famous for red embroidery on white, while Dalecarlia is known for blackwork and lace.

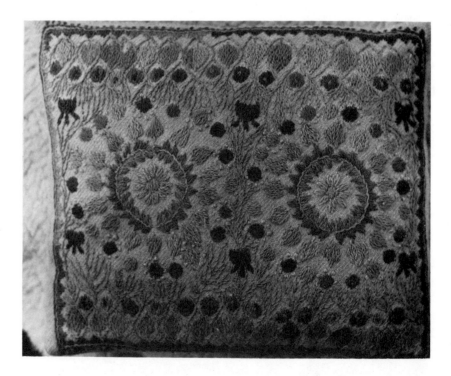

Swedish wedding pillow made from natural-dyed wool yarns on hand-woven wool fabric. The flowers, berries, and the little three-legged iron dyepot denote the source of the yarns' colors. Made for Astri Feist.

These regional variations have been encouraged since 1899 by the Swedish Handcraft Societies, whose members have made needlework and other crafts a vigorous living tradition in the country. Each society operates independently, supporting the local crafts, particularly textiles. A worker can either be commissioned for specific items, take home kits to work up, or produce a small line, which is bought directly and resold by the local Society store. Customers can also buy the kits, and if one chooses to work an intricate design, where a diagram would be too expensive to print, she borrows the original for a week to study the stitches. Quality is stressed, so that items are both beautiful and useful. The basic aim is to make something suitable to modern life, yet based in Swedish tradition.

WORKING PROCESS:
Free Embroidery on Pillow *See also color plate 11*

In Sweden children start embroidering in the first grade and continue throughout their education. Thus we designed a simple and playful piece, capable of being worked by anyone from the age of 8 on up. We chose the manner of Halsingland, with its red-on-white wool embroidery.

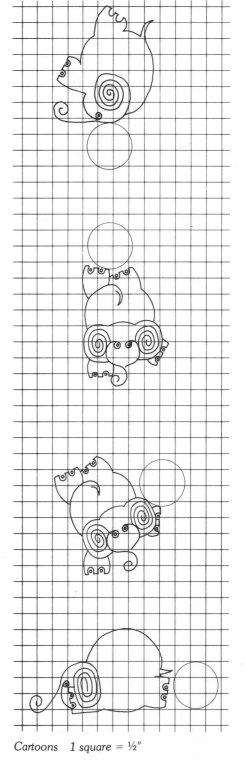

Cartoons   1 square = ½″

Project Pointers

A child can use a tapestry needle instead of an embroidery needle.
Don't pull the chain stitches too tight or the material will bump out.
Use ½″ seams throughout.

YOU WILL NEED

½ yard red wool fabric
¼ yard white wool fabric
1 skein each, wool embroidery thread: red and white (I used French wool)
14″ pillow form
embroidery or tapestry needle, scissors
doodle cloth

Chain stitch

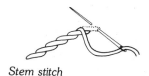

Stem stitch

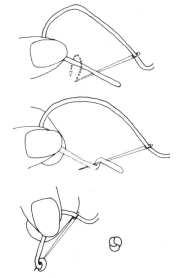

French knots

How to make tassels: Wrap yarn several times around a piece of stiff cardboard as long as you wish the tassel to be. Slip a long piece of yarn between the cardboard and the wrapped yarn, and tie off the top. Cut the other end of the wrapped yarn to remove the cardboard. To form the top of the tassel, tie a long piece of yarn around the tassel in a knot. Take one end of the yarn and wrap it around the tassel, covering the knot and the other end. Then thread the end you're wrapping with, and tuck it over the wrapped part and down into the center of the tassel.

1. Cut two 8″ squares of red wool and two of white wool. Fold each square in half vertically and lightly press in center. Transfer the elephants to the squares, positioning them 1½″ above the raw edge.

2. Stitch the elephants as shown on the cartoon. Don't pull the chain stitches too tight or the centers will pouch out. When you work the stem stitch, keep the thread to the outside of any curves. Backstitch any tiny areas (toes, tail). Be sure to notice that the back of stem stitch is backstitch and vice versa. In making the French knots, wrap the thread twice around the needle for the eyes, and only once for the toenails.

3. When done embroidering, put the elephants face down on a towel and steam-press them. Sew the top two sections together with a ½″ seam; then, the two bottom sections. Press open seams. Then carefully sew the top section to the bottom section, making sure the center seams are aligned.

4. To construct the pillow back, cut two pieces of red wool, each 9½″ × 15″. On each, turn under one 15″ edge ½″ and topstitch ¼″ from the edge. Lay one of the pieces on a flat surface, right side up. Lay the second piece, right side up, on top of it, overlapping the two turned-under edges 2″. Lay the right side of the pillow top with embroidery against the right side of the pillow back. Pin. Sew around all four sides with a ½″ seam. Clip corners and turn right side out. Press.

5. Make four tassels as shown above, two of red and two of white. Thread the ends through a tapestry needle and sew into the corners of the pillow. Reach through the pillow opening, and tie the ends securely on the inside. If they slip out, turn the pillow inside out and stitch around the corners a second time.

ADDITIONAL IDEAS

1. Stitch these funny little creatures all over a child's overalls.
2. Decorate a circus cake with icing elephants.
3. Use the same pillow idea and color scheme but stitch four small toucans from section V, Peru.

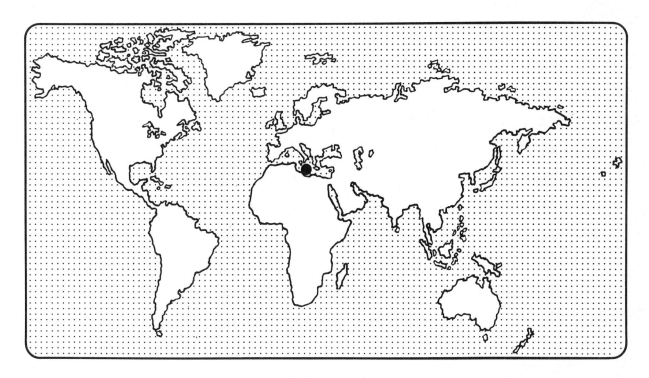

MALTA

Smack dab in the middle of the Mediterranean Sea, halfway between North Africa and Sicily, is the island of Malta, only 17 miles long and 9 miles wide. Its position has put it in the path of traders and conquerors throughout history. In fact Malta's language is supposedly the last remaining trace of a Phoenician dialect, which is amazing considering that Phoenicia disappeared as a world power before the birth of Christ. The island of Malta gained independence from Great Britain in 1964.

Although numerous cultures have filtered into Malta over the hundreds of years—and needlework shows these many different styles—the people have managed to remain little affected by the foreign influence. They merely headed for caves whenever a foreign sail came over the horizon. Caves there are and plenty of stone. Some ancient civilization shoved huge stone cubes into place for temples and then carefully rounded and curved all the corners, including those on the inside. These people disappeared suddenly.

No one is precisely sure how the raised fluffs called Maltese tufts evolved. They were used on household furnishings such as curtains, and they still bring an elegant texture into a room. In the late nineteenth century Maltese tufting was a fad that swept Europe. It is similar to the candlewick bedspreads so popular in American colonial times.

WORKING PROCESS:
Tufting on Christmas Centerpiece *See also color plate 9*

I mentioned earlier that I save thread to send in letters to friends. Another use for these thread ends is in Maltese tufts. Here we've designed a tufted Christmas centerpiece for the holiday table.

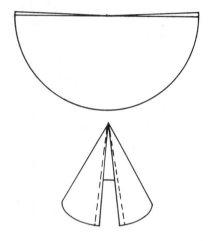

Making a cone from a semicircle

Project Pointers

Work Maltese tufts from the bottom edge up.
Work the tufts closest to the seam line after it is stitched.

YOU WILL NEED

¼ yard green felt (enough to make several centerpieces)
2 hanks green yarn (I used Persian but anything works)
2 strands each: yellow, magenta, red, and blue yarn
sewing thread and embroidery needle, scissors
tissue paper and marking pen
compass
large-eyed embroidery needle (chenille needle is perfect)
stiff paper
doodle cloth

1. Blow up and transfer the cartoon to tissue paper with the marking pen. The easiest way to do this is to make a photocopy of the cartoon. Lay the tracing paper over it and mark the center top point. Put the ruler along the lines radiating from this point and draw them 7¾" long. Then take the compass and swing a semicircle every ¾" from the outside in. Wasn't that an easy way to blow up the design!

2. Lay the tissue paper on the stiff paper and cut out the semicircle.

3. Pin the tissue paper to the green felt. With the sewing thread, baste running stitches along the line of stitching, marking each Maltese tuft with a stitch. Cut out the pattern. Carefully tear off the tissue paper.

Project photo

4. To make life easier for yourself, mark the colors on the cartoon with colored marking pens. Pretend all colors except green are colored lights and notice how they drape up and down the tree.

5. Practice the Maltese tuft stitch on your doodle cloth, using the large-eyed embroidery needle.

6. Work the tufts from the bottom up, which is the curved edge, not the straight edge. Use a double thread for all tufts except where two

Tuft Colors

◆◆ = Green

○ ○ = Yellow

◉◉ = Red

■■ = Blue

☐☐ = Magenta

Cartoon   1 square = ¼″

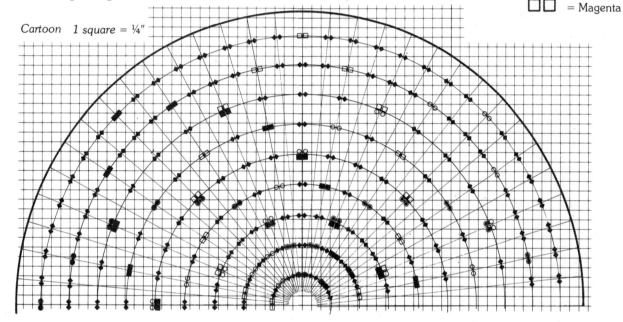

colors fall—here, thread one strand of each through the needle and hold the ends near the needle in your pinkie as shown in the Introduction. Don't pull the stitches too tight as the felt will wobble. I did not work the stitches near the seam line until after the ¼″ seam had been sewn.

7. Staple the stiff paper closed and put it under the centerpiece for support.

ADDITIONAL IDEAS

1. Expand the size of the semicircle and make a cheerful tufted sun hat for a child or yourself.
2. Bring texture to your curtains. Work large tufts of leftover knitting yarn along the border.
3. I put a small pink Maltese tuft on the seat of Tony's running shorts, but perhaps you can think of a better third idea.

Maltese tufts: Cut a thread (or threads) about 6″ long and thread the needle with it. On your basted stitch, go into the middle at A and come out at B (the left side of the basted stitch). Swing the needle around to C—go into the fabric and come out at A again. Cut the threads ends even, rethread the needle, and do another Maltese tuft

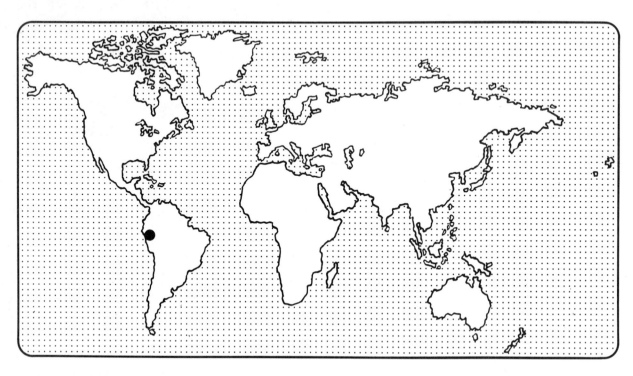

❧PERU

It has been said that by studying only pre-conquest Peruvian textiles, you could recreate almost all the needlework techniques known to humanity throughout the world. And yet scholars cannot pinpoint any contact between Peru and Asia or Europe before the Spaniards arrived in Peru in 1532. How did these marvelous people develop independently of the rest of the world?

Ancient Peru was about half the size of the United States, extending into present-day Ecuador, Bolivia, and Chile. We usually associate Peru with the Incas, but the country and its needlework were already highly developed when the Incas took over in 1200 A.D. Unfortunately there was no written language, even though the Incas introduced schools, so we have no documentation of the people who produced these mystery textiles.

By the way, the Incas had an ingenious way to remember history without writing dates. Specially trained people memorized all the important legends and facts to be passed from generation to generation. To aid their memories, they fingered "quipus," lengths of colored string knotted in code. This was a forerunner of such mnemonic devices as tying a string to your finger to remind yourself to turn off the sprinkler.

The pre-Inca people most interesting to modern needleworkers lived on the sandy coast south of the modern city of Lima. Although all around was barren desert, with little rain, the people lived in fertile valleys where small rivers joined the Pacific Ocean. Since marshes occur where land meets water and since birds love marshes, it is not surprising that the ancient Peruvians often portrayed birds in their needlework. They also embroidered fish and the great cats, like pumas, and were not averse to combining designs into bird-fish or fish-cats.

The dead were buried out in the desert sand. Operating under the assumption that you *can* take it with you, the deceased were buried with their gold and silver, as well as useful articles from daily life such as needles, spindle whorls, and such. Well-meaning relatives also tossed into the grave needlework in progress. These half-finished pieces are useful to scholars in figuring out how stitches were worked.

The reason the pieces have been preserved for those same scholars is that the textiles did not disintegrate in the dry sand. Ironically, the rich built tombs for themselves in the clay subsoil

Tiny hummingbirds of three-dimensional Peruvian loopstitch sip from flowers. The birds are no bigger than a thumb. Their beaks have disintegrated, since they are almost 1700 years old (Nasca period = about 300 A.D.). Photo courtesy of the Lowie Museum of Anthropology, University of California, Berkeley.

Project photo

because it was more permanent. But it was also moist, and artifacts rotted. Thus the textiles we study today may have belonged to the poor, but they're still of astonishing quality. The ancient Peruvian fiber has been called "the perfect thread" because of its smoothness and uniform size. How it was created is still a mystery.

The Peruvians loved fringes and tassels and doodads hanging down from their clothes. One technique of making rows of tiny whimsical three-dimensional objects—like hummingbirds sucking nectar from little flowers—has been regrettably called "needle-knitting." Since no knitting or crochet needles have ever been found in Peruvian graves, later scholars dubbed it "knit-stem." I will now muddy the waters further by calling it Peruvian loopstitch.

WORKING PROCESS:
Loopstitch Doll *See also color plate 12*

The Peruvians loved birds and dolls, and we've used this love as a basis for designing our favorite bird, the toucan. Do you need a shoulder cradle to free your hands as you talk on the telephone? His beak and bill are filled with sand, so he can hang over the shoulder. I loved working this little fellow, who became José as his brilliant tail feathers emerged. If you run out of one color, substitute another, as the Peruvians did.

> *Project Pointers*
> **Use the textile paints leftover from the Egyptian project.**

YOU WILL NEED

2 pieces of 8″ × 11″ white or off-white medium-weight fabric (I used leftover duck from the Bulgarian tote)
small amount of muslin or any odd scrap of fabric
3 jars textile paint (or use felt-tipped pens): sky blue, yellow, red
1 black fine-point felt-tipped pen
sand or bird seed
dacron or cotton batting or any stuffing material
leftover amounts of knitting or needlepoint yarn: navy blue, yellow, orange, sky blue, lime green
tapestry needle to fit yarn
doodle cloth

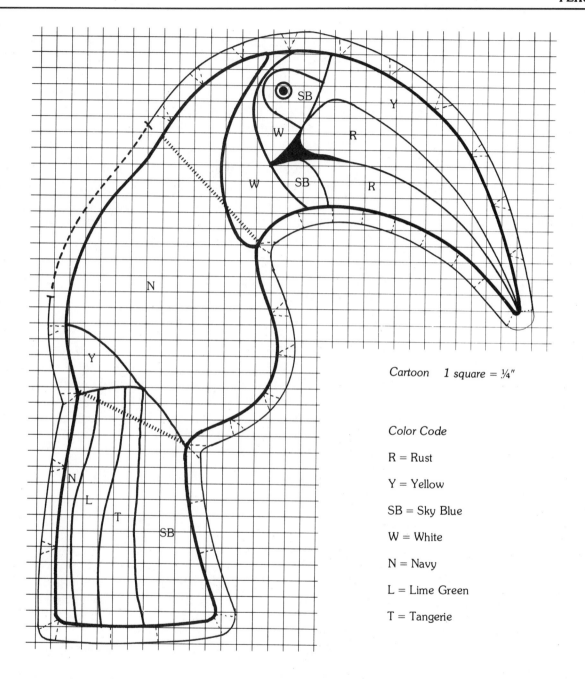

Cartoon   1 square = ¼″

Color Code

R = Rust

Y = Yellow

SB = Sky Blue

W = White

N = Navy

L = Lime Green

T = Tangerie

1. Transfer the toucan to your fabric, reversing the pattern so you have a left and right side. Don't cut the fabric yet.

2. Paint the bill with textile paint, using the colors indicated on the cartoon. After the paint has dried, set it by ironing from the back with a hot iron, as indicated on the bottle's instruction sheet.

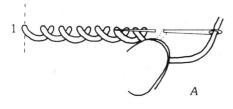

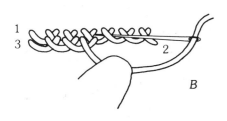

Peruvian loopstitch:
A. Work left to right. Come up at 1 and make a series of stitches across the fabric until you reach the right side. Go into the fabric at 2 and behind it, back to the left side.
B. To make the second row, loop the needle behind the threads of the row you made in A, without catching the fabric.
C. The completed second row. When you reach the right side, go into the fabric at 4 and behind it to the left side again. Always go back to the left side to start a new row. To add stitches, make an extra buttonhole stitch over the loop in the row above.

3. To make the bags that will weight the bird, cut out two bills and two·tails from muslin on the toucan stitching line. Stitch ¼″ inside this edge around three sides of both bill and tail, leaving the largest end of each open. Turn the mini-pockets inside out and fill with sand. Hand stitch the openings closed as sloppily as you wish—no one will ever see your work . . . unless an archeologist digs it up 1000 years from now.

4. Cut out both sides of the toucan. Put right sides of the bird together and stitch by hand or machine around the outline, leaving the back open as indicated on the cartoon. Clip the curves (not *too* close) as shown above, so the toucan won't look like he has middle-age bulges. Then turn right side out.

5. Insert the two sand-filled bags, stuff the rest of the little bugger with batting, and sew up the opening by hand, using the ladder stitch shown above.

6. Practice Peruvian loopstitch on a doodle cloth.

7. Work left to right, starting at the top of the head. (If your eyesight is not good, substitute a lighter-colored yarn for navy blue.) The top of the head is done in two separate sections, from the left side along the eye toward the center seam and from the center seam toward the right eye side. As soon as you have filled in the back head area even with the line under his chin, you can work in a circle all around his body. Add and drop stitches as needed.

8. At the bottom of the tail, lace the two sides of each color section together with a simple overcast stitch.

ADDITIONAL IDEAS

1. Reduce José to 4″ tall. Find a drapery fabric with large leaves or trees on it (or paint your own)—embroider in chain stitch as many little toucan outlines on it as you can handle and use for a dress, pillow, or curtains.
2. Use the Peruvian loopstitch in José's tail feather colors as a sleeve edging to transform a purchased dress from ordinary to extraordinary.
3. Punch holes by unthreaded machine or hand in heavy-weight red paper (ask at the art store for card stock) in the shape of a heart (use the one in Denmark, section J, p. 85). Use Peruvian loopstitch in hot pink to fill in the heart shape. Write a note and send to someone you love.

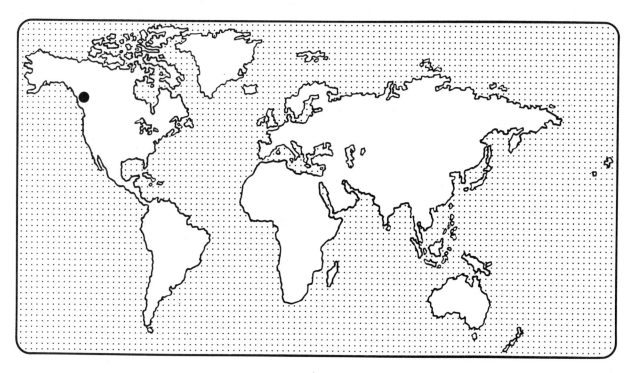

CANADA

When you live in a mild coastal climate surrounded by a big ocean (Pacific), big mountains (Coast), big trees (Douglas fir, cedar), and big fish and game (salmon and grizzlies), you tend to respond to your environment in a big way. Thus the art of the Northcoast Indians on the west coast of Canada was bold and vigorous.

Rank was everything to these people, and it was determined by family and birth. A man inherited the right to the power of his family's guardian spirits, as experienced through songs, stories, and dances. But having the right did not guarantee having the power. In order to earn the power, one had to stage a potlatch, an extravagant feast that lasted many days. All relatives plus other tribes were invited, and everybody wore their rank in the form of family crests on their clothing and blankets. These crests had been acquired in visions or by killing monsters such as whales and then carved, painted, or stitched on everything in sight.

One purpose of the potlatch was to pass on the family power, as

Kwakiutl Button Cloak, photo courtesy of The Museum of Anthropology, University of British Columbia, Vancouver

well as the family crest, so in between eating there were dramatic performances, dances, and singing. But another aspect of the potlatch was to outdo the other clans. Each group tried to prove and improve on their long, outstanding family history by displaying and giving away vast amounts of wealth. It was not a bad investment, for by the rules of the game, if you gave away 50 blankets at your potlatch, the other guy had to give you 100 blankets at his. Unfortunately whole villages went broke overnight when a chief became too enthusiastic about outdoing a neighbor.

It did create a healthy atmosphere for the arts, with all those commissions for totem poles, whaling canoes, bowls, and blankets, all to be decorated with the family crests. The use of the object was most important, and the design made to fit that.

In portraying the animals that served as family property marks, the artist accented the creature's distinctive features—for example the cross-hatching of a beaver's tail or the teeth of a shark. But they also showed the whole animal, front and back—head, ears, tail, arms, and feet. There was an aversion to empty space, and the animal was freely distorted to fill up the object. The artist could do this any way he wished, as long as the community could still understand the design.

Button blankets evolved in the eighteenth century when traders brought cloth and Hudson Bay Company blankets. Before that, the

Indians decorated the family crests with dentalium shells from the warm waters of the Queen Charlotte Islands in British Columbia. The men tattooed gauge lines on their forearms to price the shells—the longer, the more valuable. (I suppose that would be one way to measure even-weave fabric today.) When trade cloth, flannel, and pearl buttons became available, these were used instead. The number of buttons sewn on is mind-boggling: often over 3000 in a single blanket. Fortunately, today we can sew these on by machine.

Cartoon 1 square = ¼″

WORKING PROCESS:
Button Blanket *See also color plate 5*

Today we don't have potlatches, but we do have occasion to display our affiliations at football or soccer games. Since our daughter's name is Kali Koala, we chose the family totem for this modern button blanket.

Project Pointers

Place the koala according to how you will use it: at the head of the blanket for beds; halfway down the long side for ball games.

YOU WILL NEED

1 army-navy surplus blanket (or any blanket)
⅔ yard light blue flannel or felt
1 jarful of white shirt buttons from second-hand store
zigzag sewing machine
sewing machine thread: white and navy
large sheet tracing or butcher paper
cellophane tape

Project photo

1. On tracing paper blow up design until it is 20″ high and 24″ wide. Transfer the design to a rectangle of blue felt or flannel. Do not cut it out yet.

2. Fold the blanket in half to find the halfway point. (If you intend to put it on a bed rather than wear it, the design should go at the head

of the blanket.) Match the halway point of the koala to the blanket halfway point. Liberally pin the rectangle of felt in place, both inside and outside all seam lines.

3. Follow the stitching lines, using the navy thread. You can either leave the presser foot on and stitch normally—which means wrestling a lot of bulk on every turn—or free machine embroider if you're experienced. (See More Bibliography for a great book on machine embroidery.)

4. Using sharp scissors, cut close to the outer seam line. Then cut away all areas on the inside that are black on the cartoon—and be careful. I made a mistake and so could you.

5. Tape about ten buttons at a time along the outer edge. Sew the buttons on by machine right through the tape, as shown above. When done, pull off the tape and clip off the connecting threads between buttons. (I only clipped those on top.)

ADDITIONAL IDEAS

1. I plan to make a quilt for Kali, quilting the shape of the koala.
2. Do you have a college, family, or club crest that means a lot to you? Work it on a blazer and emphasize the lines with small buttons.
3. Blow up the horse design from section D, Greece, p. 54, and appliqué it to a riding jacket surrounded by buttons.

SUPPLIES AND BIBLIOGRAPHY—WOOL

Dewey Decimal library call numbers given in parentheses when known

Wool

Sommer, Elyse and Mike. *A New Look at Felt.* New York: Crown, 1975. $6.95 (746S).
American Wool Council, 200 Clayton St., Denver, CO 80206.
Black Sheep Newsletter, Rt. 2, Box 123-E, Monroe, OR 97456—$2/year.
National Wool Grower, 600 Crandell Building, Salt Lake City, UT 84101—$5/yr.
Shelburne Spinners, 2 Howard St., Burlington, VT 05401—natural-dyed hand-spun embroidery yarns, $2/skein.
Winter Creek Spinners, 2100 Mt. Diablo Scenic Blvd., Danville, CA 94526—hand-spun wool thread.
Elizabeth Zimmerman, Babcock, WI—primarily yarns for knitting plus a delightful newsletter, *Wool Gathering.*

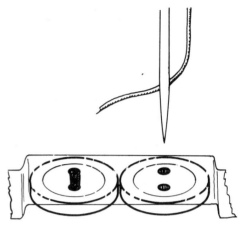

Sewing buttons on by machine: Set up the machine for free machine embroidery and if possible, decenter your needle. Cellophane tape the buttons to the blanket. Take three stitches in one hole of the button to lock the threads, then adjust the width of the zigzag so the needle will stitch back and forth between button holes. Return to no zigzag and lock threads again. Raise presser bar lever and move to next button without clipping threads. Lower presser bar lever and repeat instructions for sewing on button. Later clip threads and pull off tape.

Russia

Lindahl, David, and Knorr, Thomas. *Uzbek, The Textiles and Life of the Nomadic and Sedentary Uzbek Tribes of Central Asia.* Zoinden Druck und Verlag AG, Basel, Switzerland, May 1975.

Persia

Hicks, Jim. *The Persians.* New York. Time-Life Books, 1975.
Sulff, Hans E. *The Traditional Crafts of Persia.* Cambridge: MIT Press, 1966.
Vreeland, Herbert H. de., *Iran.* Human Relations Area Files, New Haven, 1957.

A. "Save the Last Dance for Me" by Joan Schulze, drawn thread and surface stitchery evoking the lost culture of the Indians, in one place emerging through a veil of threads; in another, hidden, waiting for discovery.

Sweden

Fisher, Eivor. *Swedish Embroidery.* Paisley, Scotland: Clark, 1953.
Handcraft in Sweden. Stockholm: LTS Forlag, 1951.

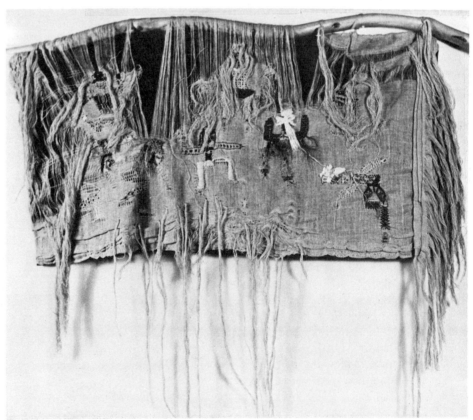

Plath, Iona. *The Decorative Arts of Sweden.* New York: Scribner's, 1948. 1948.

Swedish Handcraft Society, Sturegatan 29, 114 36 Stockholm, Sweden—*Hemslojden,* their bimonthly magazine, is $10.80/year.

Malta

Hughes, Quentin. *Fortress/Architecture and Military History in Malta.* London: Lund Humphries, 1969.

Peru

Bird, Junius. *Paracas Fabrics and Nazca Needlework.* Washington, DC: Catalogue Raisonne, 1954.

Crawford, M.D.C. "Peruvian Textiles." *Anthropological Papers of the American Museum of Natural History,* vol. 12, part 3-4, 1915.

Harcourt, Raoul d'. *Textiles of Ancient Peru and Their Techniques.* Seattle: University of Washington Press, 1962.

Canada

Appleton, LeRoy H. *American Indian Design and Decoration.* New York: Dover, 1971. $4.50.

Boas, Franz. "The Decorative Art of the Indians of the North Pacific Coast." *Bulletin.* American Museum of Natural History, 1897.

Conn, Richard. *Robes of White Shell and Sunrise.* Denver Art Museum, 1974. $7.50.

Craven, Margaret. *I Heard the Owl Call My Name.* New York: Doubleday, 1973—fiction.

Davis, Robert T. *Native Arts of the Pacific Northwest.* Stanford University Art Series, California, 1949.

Garfield, Viola E. *The Tsimshian Indians and Their Arts.* Seattle: University of Washington Press.

Embroiderers' Association of Canada, 90 East Gate, Winnipeg, Manitoba R3C 2C3 Canada—$10/year.

B. Detail

part five   SILK

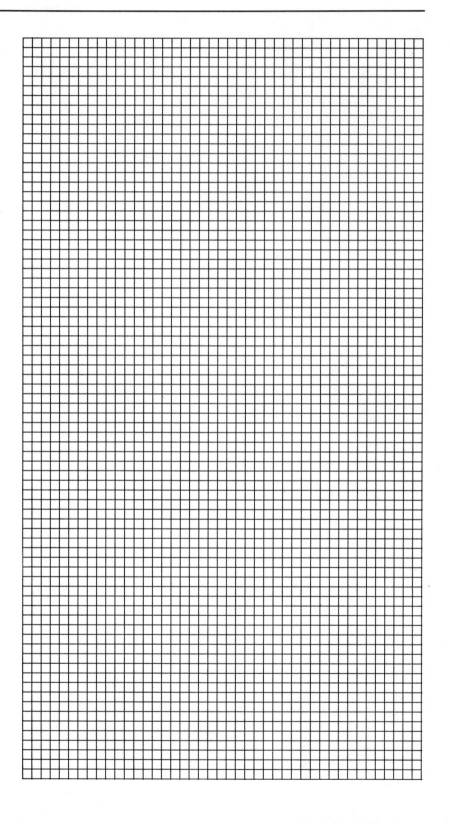

Silk has always been the fiber of mystery and romance, perhaps because of its close association with China. The wild silk moth long ago lost its powers of flight and became completely dependent on the human race for survival, but not before it threatened to defoliate the wild mulberry trees in China.

> One day in 2640 B.C. the 14-year-old Empress Hsi-Ling-Shih was walking in her royal garden when she noticed an ugly "worm" munching mulberry leaves. She didn't squish it because it might contain the spirit of a dead ancestor. Each day she watched it grow fatter, until suddenly it reared up and began to spin a soft, lustrous cocoon from its mouth. Back and forth, back and forth it waved, until finally the "worm" exhausted itself. Mistaking it for dead, Hsi-Ling-Shih carried the cocoon to her rooms in the palace. But miracle of miracles, about ten days later the "worm's" soul emerged as a moth.
>
> "Time for Your Highness' bath," commanded the court ladies, interrupting her miracle.
>
> The young Empress climbed into the hot water, still carrying her "soul prison." By accident, she dropped the cocoon into the bath. The sticky gum softened and the cocoon began to unreel a golden filament.
>
> "Oh look," said the Empress. "Organic kite string."

Since silk is already spun in the cocoon and ready for use, it did not take the Chinese long to perfect weaving and embroidery with it. Hsi-Ling-Shih's serendipitous bath discovery, the golden filament, may also have been the beginning of yellow as the imperial color. At any rate, Hsi-Ling-Shih was named the Goddess of Silkworms, and her celestial residence is the constellation Silk House, or Scorpius. For several thousand years small amounts of silk were burned every year as a sacrifice to the Goddess. Whether it is permitted today is not known.

Actually silk "worms" are a species of caterpillar, *Bombyx mori*, but the ancient Chinese deliberately misled the rest of the world about the cultivation of silk. Sericulture (production of raw silk by raising silkworms) became a royal monopoly, and the Chinese isolated themselves from Western civilization. Trade with foreigners was prohibited under penalty of death and no silk fabric, silk moth eggs, mulberry tree seeds, or even Chinese people were allowed to leave the country.

In 206 B.C. trade with Persia opened via Chinese Turkestan by way of Khotan. This first Silk Road, one of many, made China instantly wealthy because the Western world developed an immediate craving for silk. It also was the beginning of the use of metal money, as well as the establishment of banks and a foreign exchange. Before, traders had bartered directly: "I'll give you four pounds of indigo dye for fourteen yards of silk." But this was inconvenient if the indigo seller had to travel several thousand miles to the fabric store. Now he could pay with coin in one country and have his silk from another country delivered to the door of his tent. Middlemen like the Persians built up a thriving trade, yet because the Chinese kept silk culture a closely guarded secret, the Persians carried silk to the West not knowing how or from what it was made.

The West continued to lust for luxurious silk, to the growing frustration of rulers. After the fall of the Roman Empire in 476 A.D., and its division into two parts, the Eastern Empire was moved to Constantinople. Justinian took over in 527 A.D. and became its greatest ruler, but he was plagued by wars with Persia. This meant he could not buy silk for his court. In 550 A.D. Justinian bribed two Persian monks to go to China and learn the secret of silk culture. After several years, the monks made a perilous trip back to Constantinople with mulberry seeds hidden in a bamboo walking stick.

"Hey, it's not fleece that grows on a tree like they told you," said one monk. "It's an insect, not a plant."

"Fantastic," replied Justinian. "Now go back and get me some silkworm eggs."

Even with this knowledge, Chinese silk continued to be sought in great volume by the Near East and Europe until the thirteenth century. In fact, the Great Wall of China—20' high, 13' wide, and 1400 miles long—was built to protect the silk caravans from attack by the vicious Hun tribes.

As silk production moved west, so did the center of the silk trade until by the seventeenth and eighteenth centuries it wobbled back and forth between England and France, according to royal blunders like the revocation of the Edict of Nantes (see p. 46 for explanation), bad winters, and revolutions.

There was a serious attempt in colonial America to replace the tobacco industry with silk, but the farmers weren't too interested. They planted the legally required ten mulberry trees per 100 acres, but they let the silkworms also eat apple, poplar, and plum leaves, which reduced the quality and volume of the silk. England was not happy about colonial silk independence and declared that only the cocoons could be harvested, a ruling the Americans ignored. Just as George Washington was inaugurated in wool, Martha Washington made a political statement by wearing a dress of Virginia raw silk.

SEWING ON AND WITH SILK

Some people focus on the high cost per yard of silk, forgetting that paying $20 to make a blouse that lasts five years is ultimately cheaper and less time-consuming than paying $4 for a blouse that has to be replaced twice a year for five years. Silk is the strongest of all natural fibers. In the late nineteenth century a New England silk thread mill was swept away in the flood of a broken dam. For years afterwards farmers ploughed up spools and skeins of silk, slightly dirty but undamaged. Silk repels dirt and can absorb 30% of its weight in moisture without feeling wet, making it cool to wear. It feels luxurious and has a wonderful sound as it moves.

Use a size 9/10 (70) needle on your machine to sew on silk and size A silk thread. Also use silk pins, because the fatter pins leave visible holes. When machine-sewing sheer silks (by the seashore?), put tissue paper behind the fabric while stitching, and then gently rip it away when finished.

Some Forms of Silk

Fabric: **brocade, chiffon, crepe (crepe de chine, georgette, etc.), silk needlepoint gauze, organza, pongee (made of wild tussah yarn), satin, shantung, taffeta**

Thread: **sewing thread in two sizes, A (finer) for construction and B (heavier) for topstitching, silk cord, raw silk, tussah**

CARE OF SILK

In general silk should be dry-cleaned, but some silks can be gently hand-washed (no twisting or wringing) in cool or lukewarm water with mild soap. Air dry in the shade. Be sure to ask your fabric store dealer how to care for the silk you buy.

Iron on the wrong side at a medium temperature without steam (to avoid water marks).

Don't treat spots yourself, as dry-cleaning fluid can mark the fabric. Take the garment to a reputable cleaning firm.

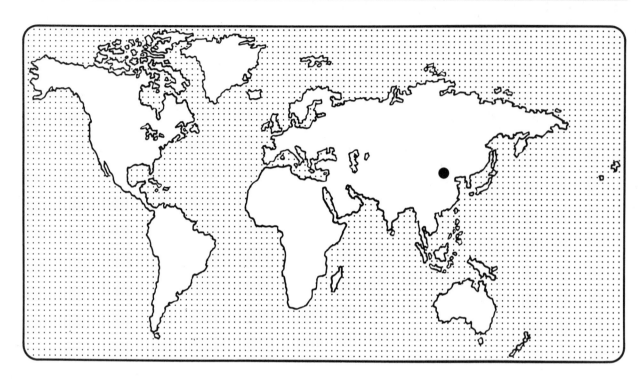

CHINA

When you stop to think about the 4000-year tradition of clothing in China—where silk was *the* textile of royalty and everyone's social rank was indicated by what (s)he wore—and then think of the simple costume worn by Chinese today, you realize that the Chinese revolution in 1947 was one of the most tremendous cultural cataclysms in history.

There were 12 symbols, each representing a larger concept, by which civil and military people announced their rank. Only the emperor, who was the go-between for the people and heaven, could wear all 12. His robe represented the entire universe, with each symbol representing a larger concept—For example, clouds represented heaven and mountains represented the earth. The 18 civil and military ranks pictured the appropriate symbols on their robes in embroidered mandarin squares, where even the buttons counted as insignia.

After the silk trade opened with the West, the Chinese began an interesting business relationship. From the fourteenth to the seventeenth centuries European churches would order embroidery on ecclesiastical garments from China. Back would come the vestment with the necessary Christian saints—surrounded by phoenixes, spotted deer, and Chinese flowers. Later the Spanish imported work from the Chinese province of Canton done in satin, split, and couching stitches, to be resold as "Spanish shawls."

Probably the most famous stitch from China was the Peking or forbidden stitch, consisting of tiny knots (similar to French knots but formed differently) completely carpeting a fabric. When too many women went blind working it, the stitch was forbidden by the Emperor.

The Chinese were very clever in working with rich fabrics, which were too expensive to ruin by mistakes. One method was to embroider separate motifs on stiff gauze or paper, then cut away the excess gauze and apply the motifs to the background fabric by embroidery or couching (*couching* means to secure thread onto a fabric by catching it down with a second thread). An interesting Chinese variation of couching was to twist two silk threads together and then couch them down. Since silk catches the light, this gave a rich texture to the work.

In 1928 the great explorer Sir Auriel Stein uncovered burial places along an ancient silk road in China. He found fragments of silk fabric, silk embroidery and sewing thread, and even silk felt dating from the fifth century B.C., making them the oldest existing

Mandarin squares were used in China to show the rank of the wearer. Each symbol stood for a level. Later the symbols, like this couched dragon, were embroidered for their own sake. Collection of the University of California, Berkeley Design Department Textile Teaching Collection.

Aries, the ram (March 21–April 20) ♈

Taurus, the bull (April 21–May 21) ♉

Gemini, the twins (May 22–June 21) ♊

Cancer, the crab (June 22–July 23) ♋

Leo, the lion (July 24– August 23) ♌

Virgo, the virgin (August 24– September 23) ♍

textiles at that time. He also found ancient temples where the people had made mini-banners of silk scraps hung from twigs.

Today we hear little about creative embroidery in China. There are institutes of embroidery and needlepoint, where glorified kits worked realistically from photographs are exported as stitch pictures to the West. These institutes are more factories than schools and do not encourage individual expression. Merely because we do not hear of it does not mean embroidery in China is dead; it's unlikely that a craft that has weathered the ups and downs of history since the beginning of humanity would die out.

WORKING PROCESS:
Couched Zodiac Sign

Today we have few ways to give the world a clue to our rank or status. Anyone may wear silk one day and overalls the next. But wearing your astronomical sign on your jacket pocket tells everybody who you are and why you tend to shut your fingers in doors or find dollar bills in gutters.

Project Pointers

Use tweezers to pluck stray threads of organza from the couched symbol.

YOU WILL NEED

1 hank silk cord or a spool of silk buttonhole twist, light blue
small square organza or organdy to fit hoop
embroidery hoop
tapestry and sewing needles, scissors
light blue sewing machine thread
purchased jacket or blazer with pocket
piece of cardboard to fit in pocket
tweezers

1. Transfer your sign to the organza.* Mount the fabric in the hoop. Thread the silk cord in the tapestry needle and start with a waste knot 4″ away from the embroidery. Bring the cord to the surface and lay it on the stitching line.

2. Thread sewing machine thread through the sewing needle. Couch the silk down, as shown above. Each symbol requires two lines of silk cord side-by-side. When you are finished, push the tapestry needle through to the back and let it hang. Cut off the waste knot but leave the long tail hanging on the back.

3. Remove the hoop. With sharp scissors cut away the organza close to the couched thread. Put the cardboard in the pocket of the jacket so you won't sew it closed. Position the symbol on the pocket, and carefully pull the tapestry needle and silk cord through the pocket. If the pocket is lined, take two backstitches through the lining to secure the thread. Thread the other tail through the needle and bring it through the pocket.

4. With the sewing thread, couch the symbol to the pocket, taking stitches halfway between the previous stitches. Use the tweezers to remove stray threads of organza.

*Note: If you are constructing the jacket from scratch, forget the organza and couch directly to the pocket before you sew it on the jacket.

Libra, the balance (September 24 – October 23) ♎

Scorpio, the scorpion and eagle (October 24 – November 22) ♏

Sagittarius, the archer (November 23 – December 21) ♐

Capricorn, the goat (December 22 – January 20) ♑

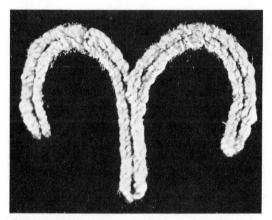

Project photo

Couching

ADDITIONAL IDEAS

1. Monogram your favorite golfer's club covers in the couching technique.
2. Couch the elephant designs from section T, Sweden, on a baby bib in pearl cotton.
3. Coil rope in spirals like the medallion in section M, West Africa, on chicken wire. Couch in place with twine and a sailmaker's needle and use for an outdoor hot pad.

Aquarius, the waterbearer (January 21 – February 19) ♒

Pisces, the fish (February 20 – March 20) ♓

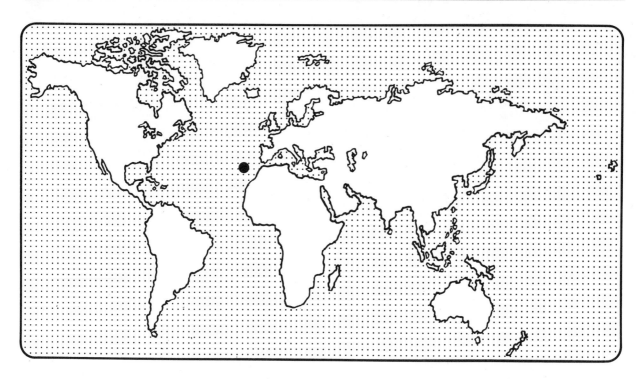

PORTUGAL (MADEIRA)

Five hundred and thirty-five miles southwest of Lisbon is a small mountainous island called Madeira. It was discovered by Columbus in the fifteenth century and named for its virgin forest (*madeira* means *wood* in Portuguese). The explorers set fire to the forest to clear a path, but the woods were so dense that the island continued to burn for seven years. This eventually made the soil remarkably fertile, and grapes for famous wine and port are produced there today.

In addition to the wine, Madeira now has two other major sources of wealth: tourists and embroidery. With an average temperature of 80°F year-round and only 80 days of rain a year, sun lovers from the north flock to the island.

All along the harbor near the big hotels are shops selling fine Madeira embroidery. These are not cheap; the government determines the price according to how many stitches are in a piece. One tablecloth may have 60,000 stitches in it and cost several hundred dollars. Proof of the successful market is that most of the island's old estates are now owned by the embroidery merchants.

The work is done by 70,000 farm women who live up in the mountains. They trudge down the lava-rock roads to the harbor to pick up fine linen and silk, which they carry back up to their homes in patchwork sewing bags. From these stout fingers come elegant, airy embroideries of fine craftsmanship.

How this industry developed is fascinating. In the mid-nineteenth century a disease threatened to destroy Madeira's only source of wealth, the vineyards. The daughter of a wine shipper, a Miss Phelps, was aware of the fine quality work of the peasants on their less than fine fabric. She took embroidery samples to London and convinced someone that a market could be created for the peasant work, if the quality of the materials improved. She brought back fine cambric linen from Scotland and Belgium, silks from France and Switzerland. Before long two major kinds of embroidery had developed—cut-work on linen and shadow appliqué on silk.

WORKING PROCESS:
Shadow Appliqué Curtains *See also color plate 6*

To commemorate the Madeira Island climate and to introduce you to shadow appliqué, we've designed a rising sun for a set of curtains.

Project Pointers

Tape the appliqués in place; pins would make holes.
Use a sewing needle for shadow stitching and a tapestry
  needle for pin stitch.

Project photo (designed by the authors, worked by Margaret Vaile)

YOU WILL NEED

enough white silk organza to fit your window (measure it before
  buying) and extra for the appliqués
1 spool size A silk thread, white
pencil, ruler, cellophane tape
tapestry and sewing needles, scissors
doodle cloth

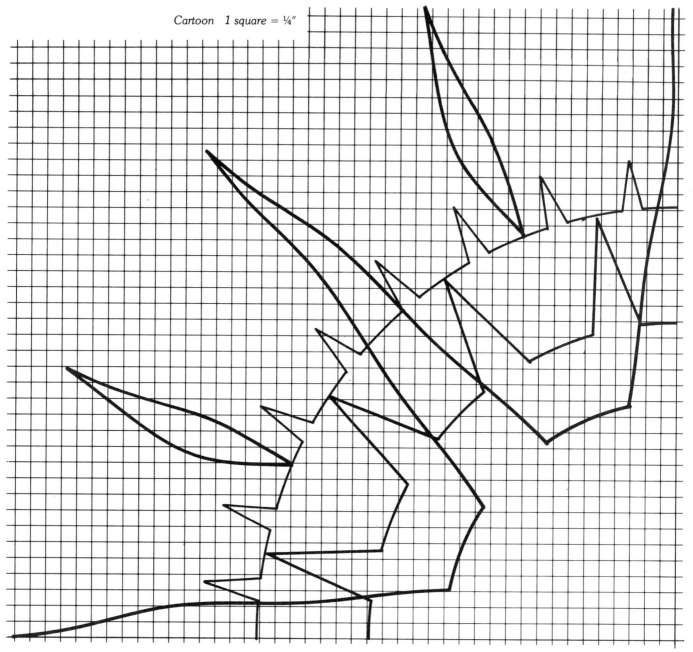

Cartoon   1 square = ¼″

1. Cut a piece of organza to fit your window, allowing 3¼″ for the top and bottom hems and ½″ for the side hems. (If you wish the curtains to part in the middle, add ½″ to each side of the split.)

2. Blow up the design to fit your curtains. Ours is 22″ wide and 11½″ high.

3. Practice shadow and pin stitching on your doodle cloth.

4. You will work the sun from the largest semicircle to the smallest in steps. Find the vertical halfway point of the curtains and lightly press. Draw a light pencil line 6¼″ from and parallel to the bottom edge of the curtain. Now lay the curtain over the cartoon and line up the bottom and middle lines of the design. Lightly trace the outside semicircle and the rays that go out from it. This is the back side of the curtain.

5. With the size A silk thread and sewing needle, shadow stitch the rays. Begin and end threads by winding them along the edges of the herringbone stitches. Don't forget that shadow stitching is done on the pencilled back side of the curtains.

6. Cut a rectangle of organza big enough for the largest semicircle. Fold it in half to find the vertical halfway line and lightly press. Lightly trace the largest semicircle with the pencil, including the shadow-stitched rays that fall on it and the line of the second largest semicircle. Shadow stitch the rays on the pencilled side. Cut out the semicircle all around with a ¼″ seam allowance. Clip the curves and press under the seam allowance. Tape, not pin, the semicircle to the curtain and pin stitch in place, as shown above, using a tapestry needle.

7. Cut another rectangle of organza the size of the second largest semicircle and trace its outline. Cut it out with a ¼″ seam allowance and pin stitch, as in step 6.

8. Transfer and cut out the smallest semicircle with the rays coming out of it, adding ¼″ seam allowance. When you position it on the curtain, line up the rays with the shadow-stitched rays. Pin stitch.

9. To hem the curtains, press ¼″ on all sides toward the *top,* not back, side of the curtain. For the bottom and top hems, turn up another 3″ and pin stitch in place. For the sides turn in an additional ¼″ and pin stitch.

ADDITIONAL IDEAS

1. Use the Persian design (section S) on a white organza blouse, shadow stitching and appliquéing the front of it.
2. Silk organza is also used for silkscreening, which is very easy to do. See the bibliography in the back of the book for a book that will teach you to transfer the Swedish elephants (section T) to a screen to make T-shirts, cards, etc.
3. Reduce the size of the sun and make a mola for a small cosmetic purse.

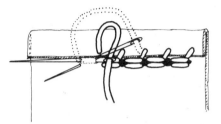

Pin stitch: A. Working right to left with a tapestry needle, make two backstitches in the curtain (about ⅜″ long).

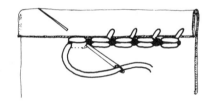

B. Come out in the hem above the left side of the last back stitch taken. Then go into the hole on the curtain directly below and repeat A.

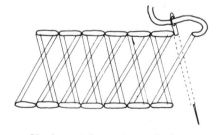

Shadow stitch can be worked as a double backstitch on the topside or as close herringbone on the backside.

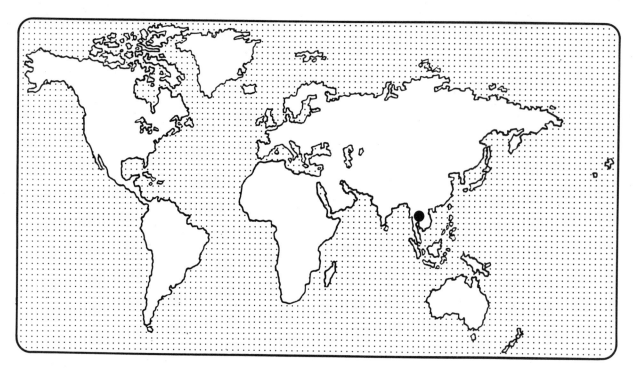

THAILAND

Many of today's Thai customs come from the time when the country was still known as Siam. For example, many women there still wear very short hair because once, long ago when the Thai men were losing one of their numerous battles, the women dressed as men, cut their hair short, and saved the day.

A current English phrase also comes from the famous white elephants of royal Siam. These animals are sacred, and it is forbidden to harm them. Long ago when a courtier displeased the king, he was given a white elephant. It was an honor to receive one and a sin to refuse one, but the useless elephant was expensive to care for and the courtier would often go broke. From this quaint custom came the phrase ''white elephant,'' which now means any possession that's more trouble than it's worth.

After World War II an American architect named Jim Thompson was wandering along the klongs (canals) of Bangkok, when he noticed an exquisite display of fabric. It was Thai silk, made with a different color for warp and weft, which imparts a gorgeous luster to the fabric. Thompson took samples of the silk back to New York and convinced *Vogue Magazine* to feature it. This was the birth of the Thai silk industry. Although sales were slow in the beginning, in 1951 they zoomed. That was the year Irene Shareff used Thai silk for the costumes in Rodgers and Hammerstein's *The King and I.*

As noted earlier, silk has always had mystery and intrigue as companions. In the 1960's Jim Thompson disappeared while on vacation in Burma. He was never found.

Raw silk is raised outside of Bangkok on small farms, some of less than an acre. Silk production takes patience and time. It can take up to 35 days to make enough silk for one dress, which explains the expense of yardage.

Further north are found hill tribes that have only been in Thailand the last 100 years. (Only! In California anybody here ten years is a native.) They came from China and Laos and are called Meo by the Thais but Hmong by themselves. "Hmong" means both "embroidery" and "free man," a pleasant combination. It has been suggested that Meo (or Miao or Meau) refers either to their catlike language or their feline ability to climb around in the mountains. To people in flight, the only way to preserve an ancient culture is to wear it, so both Meo men and women wear handsome cross-stitched costumes edged with strips of appliqué. Luckily, some of this wonderful embroidery is exported.

Bag from Meo of Thailand—Meo appliqué on top flap with cross stitch below. Contrary to often-repeated information, not all cross stitch is crossed in the same direction. The Meo meticulously cross every other stitch the same, both vertically and horizontally. This gives the appearance of a four-sided stitch on the back. Collection of Sas Colby.

WORKING PROCESS:
Meo Appliqué Needlecase *See also color plate 8*

Combining Thai silk with Meo appliqué, we've designed the needlecase that you needed way back at the beginning of this book.

Project Pointers

Do not pin silk where it will show; use cellophane tape.

YOU WILL NEED

typing-weight scrap paper or graph paper
10″ × 7″ piece orange Thai silk (¼ yard is enough for three needlecases)
small amount black and pink Thai silk or any lightweight fabric

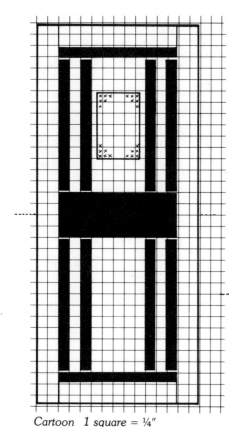

Cartoon   1 square = ¼"

two rectangles of felt, each 8½" × 3¾"
silk thread, either size D buttonhole twist or one of the new imported Japanese threads (ask your favorite needlework shop owner or see Silk Supplies and Bibliography)
sewing machine, with orange sewing machine thread on bobbin
embroidery needle, hoop
10" narrow ribbon
ruler

1. Cut the main pattern pieces out of typing-weight scrap paper (or graph paper). Label them and use as patterns to cut the fabric accurately.
    1 piece orange Thai silk, 10" × 5¼"
    4 black strips, each ¾" × 8½"
    2 orange strips, each ¾" × 8½"
    1 black strip, 1½" × 3¾"
    2 black strips, ¾" × 3¾"
    2 pieces of felt, each 8½" × 3¾"
    1 pink rectangle, 1½" × 1"

2. You will begin by appliquéing the center pink rectangle. Place the piece of paper you cut for it on the wrong side of your fabric. Do not use pins—tape it to the fabric. Cut ¼" around the paper. Turn in the edges of the fabric around the paper. Catch stitch the four corners together. Press lightly with an iron set to a low temperature, no steam. Now remove the paper.

3. Cut the large rectangle of Thai silk, which is the base for the needlecase. Fold the wrong sides together, and mark the fold line with your iron; then open it out flat again. The pink rectangle should be placed 2⅛" in from the three front edges (1⅜" from the fold). Sew it in place along the edge, taking tiny overcast stitches.

4. Using the embroidery silk and the embroidery needle, make the set of cross stitches in each corner of the rectangle. Either use a transfer pencil to mark the fabric or, easier, eyeball it. If you would like to monogram the needlecase, do it now. Use the letters that start each section in this book. (I worked my initial in backstitch, using a hoop.) Start and end threads behind the pink rectangle on the orange silk—these stitches will soon be covered.

5. Cut the two pieces of felt. Put one of them against the wrong side of the orange silk, which should be ¾" larger all around than the felt. Pin in place only near the edges of the felt. The pinholes will later be covered.

6. Fold all the black and orange strips in half lengthwise and press.

Take one of the black strips and place it along the entire top edge of the needlecase (front and back), so the black fold runs 2" from the top edge of the orange silk and points toward the center. The black strips run from one end of the felt to the other; therefore ¾" of orange silk will stick out on each end. Pin in place near the raw edges of the black. Sew by hand or machine ⅛" from the raw edge, starting and stopping exactly at the felt. Secure threads by back stitching.

7. Repeat step #6 exactly for the bottom edge of the black, through black/orange silk/felt.

8. Lay the edge of the orange strip so the fold lies on the black seam line. Stitch both top and bottom as in step 6.

9. Lay the two short black strips across each end, folds pointing toward the center, 1½" from the ends of the orange silk. Stitch ⅛" from the raw edges, starting and ending exactly at the felt.

10. Put the second piece of felt inside the needlecase, and pin in place through the felt only. Stitch through all three layers down the center fold you ironed earlier, starting and ending exactly at the felt.

11. Turn ¼" in on the two long edges of the remaining black strip and press. Place over the center line you stitched in step 10 and hand stitch to the orange silk on each side.

12. Fold the outer edge of orange silk ¾" in to the *outside* of the needlecase. Press. Then press under ¼". Hand stitch the two ends first. The orange fold should fall on the stitching line of the black strips all around. Now hand stitch the two long orange folds in place, using a ladder stitch on the corner edges and an overcast stitch everywhere else.

13. If the felt sticks out anywhere, trim it.

Project photo

14. Cut the ribbon in two. Sew each half to the edges of the needle-case. Now you can keep all your tapestry needles separate from your embroidery needles.

ADDITIONAL IDEAS:

1. If you can buy remnants of silk, make a needlecase using the Eskimo wallet cartoon (section A).
2. Make a purse with Meo appliqué at the top and the Uzbek design (section R) in cross stitch in the center.
3. Surely you're full of ideas by now—good luck with your own folk embroidery and appliqué.

"Kimono for Anais Nin" by Sas Colby, interprets scenes from Nin's prose-poem, "House of Incest:" "Lost in the colors of the Atlantide, the colors running into one another without frontiers. Fishes made of velvet, of organdie with lace fangs, made of spangled taffeta, of silks and feathers. . . ."— words stitched in silk on silk and hung with glass beads. Photo courtesy of Folkwear Ethnic Patterns.

SUPPLIES AND BIBLIOGRAPHY—SILK

Dewey Decimal library call numbers given in parentheses when known

Silk

Boulger, G. S. *The History of Silk,* London: East and West, 1920.

I Am Japan Raw Silk. The Central Raw Silk Association of Japan, Tokyo, 1933.

Leggett, William F. *The Story of Silk,* J. J. Little and Ives Co., 1949.

Silk, Its Origin, Culture and Manufacture. The Corticelli Silk Mills, 1911.

Cheryl Kolander, Myrtle Creek, OR—silk cords and thread, raw silk, $2 for color charts.

Thai Silks, 393 Main Street, Los Altos, CA 94022—25¢ for listing of fabric, scarves, embroidered garments, batiks, cotton, Swiss linen— wonderful place.

Yarn Loft Imports, P. O. Box 771, Del Mar, CA 92014—several weights of Japanese embroidery silk, 50¢ for color sheet.

China

Fairservis, Walter A., Jr. *Costumes of the East.* Old Greenwich, CT: Chatham, 1972. $15 (391F).

Priest, Alan, and Simmons, Pauline. *Chinese Textiles.* Metropolitan Museum of Art, New York 1931.

Portugal

Dervenn, Claude. *Madeira.* Paris: Horizons de France.

Thailand

Moore, Frank J. *Thailand,* New Haven, CT: Hraf Press, 1974.

Newman, Thelma R. *Contemporary Southeast Asian Arts and Crafts.* New York: Crown, 1977. $7.95 (745.5N)

Thai Silk. Thai Export Bulletin #3, Bangkok, 1965.

Walker, Anthony R. *Farmers in the Hills.* Penang: Universiti Sains Malaysia, 1975.

Young, Gordon. *The Hills Tribes of Northern Thailand.* Bangkok: The Siam Society, 1962.

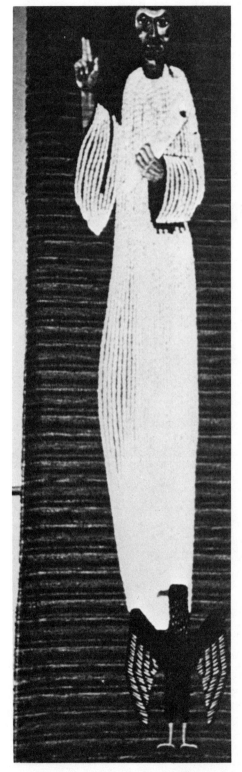

"St. John the Evangelist" by Eleanor Van de Water, commission for Newman Center, Pocatello, Idaho—couching for the robe, surface stitchery for face, hands and eagle, 4' × 36'.

RESOURCES

GROUPS INTERESTED IN NEEDLEWORK

Center for the History of American Needlework
P.O. Box 8162
Pittsburgh, PA 15217
$10 contribution, quarterly newsletter

National Standards Council of American Embroiderers
c/o Mrs. W. R. Thrailkill
12920 N.E. 32nd Pl.
Bellevue, WA 98005
$10/year, *Flying Needle* quarterly magazine

Embroiderer's Guild of America
6 E. 45th St.
New York, NY 10017
$12/year, *Needle Arts* quarterly magazine

American Crafts Council
44 W. 53rd St.

New York, NY 10019
$18/year, *Crafts Horizons* bimonthly magazine

Counted Thread Society
3305 S. Newport St.
Denver, CO 80224
$3/year, quarterly magazine

American Needlepoint Guild
PO Box 4423
Charlotte, NC 28204
$7.50/year

Textile Museum
2320 S. Street NW
Washington, DC 20008
quarterly magazine, write for price

MAGAZINES SPECIALIZING IN NEEDLEWORK

Fiber

Fiberarts
    3717 4th St NW
    Albuquerque, NM 87107
    $9/year, bimonthly

Interweave
    2938 N. County Rd. 12
    Loveland, CO 80537
    $8/year, quarterly

Open Chain
    P.O. Box 2634
    Menlo Park, CA 94025
    $1, single copies only

Quilts

Canada Quilts
    360 Stewart Dr.
    Sudbury, Ontario P3E 2RS CANADA
    $5.50 USA, 5 issues a year

Quilter's Newsletter
    Box 394
    Wheatridge, CO 80033
    $7/year, 11 issues

Needlepoint

National Needlework News
    171 Guadalupe
    Sonoma, CA 95476
    $3.50/year, biannual for shopowners

Needlepoint Bulletin
    50 South US 1, Suite 200
    Jupiter, FL 33458
    $12/year, bimonthly

Needlepoint News
    Box 668
    Evanston, IL 60204
    $7/year, bimonthly

OTHER CRAFT MAGAZINES OF INTEREST TO NEEDLEWORKERS

Crafts 'n Things
    14 Main St
    Park Ridge, IL 60068
    $5/year, bimonthly

The Crafts Report
    801 Wilmington Trust Bldg.
    Wilmington, DE 19801
    $13.50/year, monthly

Creative Crafts
    P.O. Box 700
    Newton, NY 07860
    $6/year, bimonthly

Decorating and Craft Ideas Made Easy
    1303 Foch

Ft. Worth, TX 76107
    $8/year, monthly except January and July

The Goodfellow Review of Crafts
    P.O. Box 4520
    Berkeley, CA 94704
    $6/year, bimonthly

Sew Business
    1271 Avenue of the Americas, Suite 3560
    New York, NY 10020
    $7/year, monthly

The Working Craftsman
    Box 42
    Northbrook, IL 60062
    $9/year, quarterly

ARTISTS

These are the artists whose work has been pictured in this book. All accept commissions and teach/lecture nationally.

Pat Ackor, 2261 North Beachwood, Apt. 3, Hollywood, CA 90068
Sas Colby, 2808 Ellsworth St., Berkeley, CA 94705
Robbie and Tony Fanning, P.O. Box 2634, Menlo Park, CA 94025
Jody House, 1021 Columbia Pl., Davis, CA 95616
K. Lee Manuel, 139 Bohren Rd., Santa Cruz, CA 95065
Bea Miller, 280 Quinhill Ave., Los Altos, CA 94022
Ann Spiess Mills, 2276 Calle Cuesta, Santa Fe, NM 87501
Joan Schulze, 808 Piper Ave., Sunnyvale, CA 94087
Wilcke Smith, 3616 Dakota NE, Albuquerque, NM 87110
Eleanor Van de Water, 11016 N.W. 21st Ave., Vancouver, WA 98665
Yvonne Porcella, 3619 Shoemake, Modesto, CA 95351

MORE BIBLIOGRAPHY

Dewey Decimal library call numbers given in parentheses when known

How-to

Anchor Manual of Needlework. Newton Centre, MA: Charles T. Branford, 1958. $12.50 (746A).

Dillmont, Th. de. *The Complete Encyclopedia of Needlework.* Philadelphia, PA: Running Press, 1972. $4.95.

Enthoven, Jacqueline. *The Stitches of Creative Embroidery.* New York: Van Nostrand Reinhold, 1964. $7.95.

Fanning, Robbie. *Decorative Machine Stitchery.* New York: Butterick, 1976. $9.95 (746.5F).

Fry, Gladys Windsor. *Embroidery and Needlework.* London: Sir Isaac Pitman, 1935.

Howard, Constance. *Inspiration for Embroidery.* London: B. T. Batsford, 1966.

Klickmann, Flora. *The Cult of the Needle.* Published by *The Girl's Own Paper and Woman's Magazine.*

Messent, Jan. *Designing for Needlepoint and Embroidery from Ancient and Primitive Sources.* New York: Macmillan, 1976. $14.95 (746.4M).

Valentino, Richard, and Mufson, Phyllis. *Fabric Printing: Screen Method.* Los Angeles: Bay Books, 1975. $3.95.

Wilson, Erica. *Embroidery Book.* New York: Scribner's 1973. $14.95.

Historical textiles

"A Romantic History of Ancient Textile Fibers," *American Fabrics Magazine,* winter 1962.

Bath, Virginia Churchill. *Embroidery Masterworks.* Chicago: Henry Regnery, 1972. $15 (q746.4B).

Birrell, Verla. *The Textile Arts.* New York: Schocken, 1973. $7.95.

Clabburn, Pamela. *The Needleworker's Dictionary.* New York: William Morrow, 1976. $19.95.

Clarke, Leslie J. *The Craftsman in Textiles.* New York: Praeger, 1968.

Gostelow, Mary. *A World of Embroidery.* New York. Scribner's, 1975, $20.

Holmes, William H. "A Study of the Textile Art in its Relation to the Development of Form and Ornament." *Sixth Annual Report of U.S. Bureau of Ethnology,* Smithsonian Institute, Washington DC, 1888.

Jones, Mary Eirwen. *A History of Western Embroidery.* New York: Watson-Guptill, 1969. $15.

Kluger, Phyllis, *A Needlepoint Gallery of Patterns from the Past.* New York: Knopf, 1975. $15 (q746.44K).

Lefebure, Ernest. *Embroidery and Lace.* H. Grevel, 1888.

Lubell, Cecil. *Textile Collections of the World.* Vols. 1 and 2. New York: Van Nostrand Reinhold, 1976. $30 and $25, respectively.

Markrich, Lilo. *Principles of the Stitch.* Chicago: Henry Regnery 1976. $7.95.

Schuette, Marie, and Muller-Christensen, Sigrid. *A Pictorial History of Embroidery.* New York: Praeger, 1963. $27.50.

Symonds, Mary, and Preece, Louisa. *Needlework Through the Ages.* London: Hodder & Stoughton, 1928.

Walton, Perry. *The Story of Textiles.* New York: Tudor, 1925.

Ornament and Symbols

Alviella, Count Goblet d'. *The Migration of Symbols.* University Books, 1894.

Binder, Pearl. *Magic Symbols of the World.*

Downer, Marion. *The Story of Design.* New York: Lothrop Lee & Shepard, 1963. $4.95 (q745D).

Glazier, Richard. *A Manual of Historic Ornament.* London: B. T. Batsford, 1906.

Hall, James. Dictionary of Subjects and Symbols in Art. New York: Harper & Row, 1974. $12.50 (R704H).

Jung, Carl G. *Man and His Symbols.* New York: Doubleday, 1964. $5.95 (q153J).

Ware, Dora, and Stafford, Maureen. *An Illustrated Dictionary of Ornament.* London: George Allen and Unwin, 1974.

Costume

Bossert, Helmuth th. *Peasant Art of Europe and Asia.* New York: Praeger, 1959.

Crawford, M. D. C. *One World of Fashion.* New York: Fairchild, 1946.

Crawford, M. D. C. *The Influence of Invention on Civilization.* Cleveland OH: World, 1938.

Fairservis, Walter A., Jr. *Costumes of the East.* Old Greenwich, CT: Chatham, 1972. $15 (391F).

Mann, Kathleen. *Peasant Costume in Europe.* New York: Macmillan, 1931.

Rudofsky, Bernard. *Are Clothes Modern?* Paul Theobald, 1947.

Tilke, Max. *Costume Patterns and Designs.* New York: Praeger, 1957. (Rq391T).

Early History

Hawkes, Jacquetta. *The Atlas of Early Man.* New York: St. Martin's Press, 1976. $15 (q930H).

Roberts, Gail. *Atlas of Discovery.* New York: Crown, 1973. $9.95 (q911R).

ACKNOWLEDGMENTS

Thanks to

Kali Koala Fanning for being

Pat and Roberta Losey Patterson and Mary M. Losey for invaluable child monitoring engineering

Steve Sokolow and Finnegan Corporation for computer help

Pat Bliss, Alberta Humphreys, and Margaret Vaile for magic fingers

all our other special patient friends and family

Cate Keller and Blanche Shoemake for cheerful secretarial help

Elyse Sommer for everything

and the following people:

Antonio Pinto Machado, Consul General of the Portuguese Consulate, San Francisco; Astri Feist, weaver; Pat Charley of the University of California at Berkeley's Program in Visual Design; Frank A. Norick, Barbara Busch, and Gene Prince of the Lowie Museum of Anthropology, UC/Berkeley; Sas Colby, Berkeley artist; Diane Leone of the Quilting Bee; Kimi Toshing, translator; Pat Bellamy and Harriet Jedlicka of The Dollhouse Factory; and Lars Speyer, our color photographer.

ANOTHER MAIL-ORDER SUPPLY LIST
(catalog price in parentheses; otherwise free — send pre-addressed stamped envelope and mention this book)

EAST COAST	THREADS						FABRICS					hoops, frames	books	art supplies	misc supplies	other
	linen	cotton	wool	silk	metal	other	aida	Har-danger	even-weave	canvas	other					
CM Almy & Son, Inc. 37 Purchase St. Rye, NY 10580 ($1)		✓		✓	✓				✓							ecclesiastical supplies transfer patterns
American Crewel and Canvas Studio PO Box 298 Boonton, NJ 07005 ($1)	✓	✓	✓	✓			✓	✓	✓	✓	wool even-weave	✓			✓	lamps, hot iron transfers
Appleton Bros. of London West Main Rd Little Compton, RI 02837			✓													
CJ Bates & Son, Inc. Chester, Ct.												✓				needles
Belding Lily Company PO Box 88 Shelby, NC 28150 (50¢)	✓	✓	✓							✓						
Book Barn PO Box 256 Avon, Ct. 06001													✓			
Cooper-Hewitt Museum Textile Dept 2 East 91st St New York, NY 10028																slide kits for sale
The Craft Gallery and Stitchery, Ltd. 96 South Broadway South Nyack, NY 10960 ($1)	✓	✓	✓	✓	✓		✓	✓	✓	✓		✓	✓		✓	sample package of threads
Cross Stitch Country PO Box 825 Pawley's Island, SC 29585							✓	✓								graphs, kits
Dover Publications 180 Varick St New York, NY 10014													✓			
Earth Guild, Inc. Hot Springs, NC 28743 ($2)		✓	✓	✓						✓					✓	starter kit
Elly PO Box 3898 New Haven, Ct. 06525 ($1)												✓	✓	graph paper	✓	clever aids
Felker Art-Needlework, Inc. 640 Valley Brook Rd Decatur, Georgia 30033	✓	✓	✓		✓	rayon floss	✓	✓	✓	✓	waste canvas, silk	✓	✓		needles, scissors	purse clasps
The Golden Eye Box 205 Chestnut Hill, Mass. 02167 ($1)		✓							✓	✓	satin	✓	✓	graph paper	✓	hot iron transfers
Just Brass, Inc. 21 Filmore Place Freeport, NY 11520 ($2)																buckles
Needle-Ease 81 Uplands Dr West Hartford, Ct. 06107												✓				
The Needlework Shop Royal Ridge Mall Nashua, NH 03060 ($1)	✓	✓	✓	✓			✓	✓	✓	✓	wool even-weave					
New World Books 2 Cains Rd Suffern, NY 10901													✓			
Out of the Past Mary Thomas Cash 1342 Harvard Rd, NE Atlanta, Ge. 30306																charts for counted thread
Pursenalities, Inc. 1619 Grand Ave Baldwin, NY 11510														graph paper		perforated paper, purse clasps
The Sewing Corner 150-11 14th Ave Whitestone, NY 11357															✓	collectible thimbles
Stanley-Berroco, Inc. 140 Mendon St Uxbridge, Mass. 01569 ($5/yarnset)			✓													novelty yarns
Sudberry House Box 421 Old Lyme, Ct. 06371																yarn palette, trays, accessories

ANOTHER MAIL-ORDER SUPPLY LIST (*Continued*)

| | THREADS | | | | | | FABRICS | | | | | | | | | |
	linen	cotton	wool	silk	metal	other	aida	Har-danger	even-weave	canvas	other	hoops, frames	books	art supplies	misc supplies	other
William Unger & Co 230 Fifth Ave New York, NY 10001			✔	✔												
The Unicorn Box 645 Rockville, Md. 20851 (50¢)													✔			
Elsa Williams, Inc. 445 Main St. West Townsend, Mass. 01474 ($1)		✔		✔						✔		✔	✔		✔	
Erica Wilson 717 Madison Avenue New York, NY 10021 ($1)		✔	✔	✔					✔	✔		✔	✔		✔	custom services
MID- AND SOUTH-WEST																
Dick Blick Company PO Box 1267 Galesburg, Ill. ($1)		✔	✔								felt	✔		✔	✔	opaque projector
Chaparral 2505 River Oaks Blvd Houston, Tx. 77019	✔	✔	✔	✔	✔		✔	✔	✔	✔	silk gauze	✔	✔		✔	Russian punch needles shisha, 100% wool felt
Fabdec 3553 Old Post Rd San Angelo, Tx. 76901																textile paints
Herschners Needlecrafts Hoover Rd Stevens Point, Wisc. 54481		✔	✔						✔		felt	✔			✔	
LeeWards Elgin, Ill. 60120		✔	✔						✔			✔			✔	
Merribee Co. Box 9680 Fort Worth, Tx. 75107		✔	✔						✔			✔			✔	
Paces Big Eye Needle Paces Ltd. Albuquerque, NM 87112																special easy-thread needle
WEST COAST																
Aardvark Adventures in Handcrafts 1191 Bannock St. Livermore, Ca. 94550			✔	✔	✔	rayon			✔			✔	✔		✔	Russian embroidery needles, 4 sizes shisha
Dharma Trading Company PO Box 9165 San Rafael, Ca. 94902																textile paints, dyes
Dirls PO Box 1499 Covina, Ca. 91722												✔				
The Dollhouse Factory 1045 Merrill St Menlo Park, Ca. 94025																supplies for miniatures
Folklorico Yarn Company PO Box 626 Palo Alto, Ca. 94301 ($2)		✔	✔	✔	✔	machine embroidery										
Folkwear Ethnic Patterns Box 98 Forestville, Ca. 95436																ethnic clothing patterns
Gemline Frame Co. 1000 E. Macy St Los Angeles, Ca. 90033												✔				stretcher bars
Leonida's Embroidery Studio, Ltd. 301-99 Osborne St. Winnipeg, Manitoba R3L 2R4 Canada (50¢)	✔	✔	✔	✔		velvet		linen and cotton	✔	✔	wool twill	✔	✔		✔	vanishing muslin
Naturalcraft, Inc. 2199 Bancroft Way Berkeley, Ca. 94704 ($1)	✔															feathers, beads, bones
The Needlecraft Shop, Inc. 4501 Van Nuys Blvd Sherman Oaks, Ca. 91403		✔	✔	✔	✔	machine embroidery	✔	cotton and linen	✔		wool even-weave		✔			hot iron transfers
Irma Schwabel 437 Kipling St Palo Alto, Ca. 94301																trims, buttons, notions

ANOTHER MAIL-ORDER SUPPLY LIST (*Continued*)

	THREADS						FABRICS									
	linen	cotton	wool	silk	metal	other	aida	Har-danger	even-weave	canvas	other	hoops, frames	books	art supplies	misc supplies	other
Status Thimble 311 Primrose Rd Burlingame, Ca.	✔	✔	✔	✔	✔		✔	✔	✔	✔		✔	✔	✔	✔	
Thumbelina Needlework Shop 1685 Copenhagen Dr. Solvang, Ca. 93463 (50¢)		✔	✔	✔	✔	rayon	✔	✔	✔	✔	silk gauze		✔		✔	
The Yarn Depot 545 Sutter St San Francisco, Ca. 94102 ($1)	✔	✔	✔	✔						✔			✔			goodie bags of yarn

INDEX

Numbers in *italics* refer to pages on which illustrations appear